First-Time Mothers, Last-Chance Babies

First-Time Mothers, Last-Chance Babies

Parenting at 35+

by Madelyn Cain

New
Horizon
Press

Far Hills,
New Jersey

Requests for permission should be addressed to:
New Horizon Press
P.O. Box 669
Far Hills, NJ 07931

Cain, Madelyn.
    First-time mothers, last-chance babies: parenting at 35+

Library of Congress Catalog Card Number: 93-84533

ISBN: 0-88282-086-9 (hc)
ISBN: 0-88282-083-4 (pb)
New Horizon Press

Manufactured in the U.S.A.

1998 1997 1996 1995 1994 / 5 4 3 2

*For Paul, who made my dream come true,
and for Elizabeth, who is that dream.*

Author's Note

This book is based on both my experience and a survey of older mothers. In order to protect the identity of others, I have changed some people's names and identifying characteristics.

Acknowledgments

This book was a collaborative effort, and I wish to thank all who made it possible.

First and foremost to Susan, the godmother of this book, who turned to me one day, asked, "Whatever happened to that book on older parenting?" and nudged me to try again. My deepest thanks.

To Paul Mantee, who supported my fledgling beginnings and made me feel I could do it. You can be the godfather.

To Joan Dunphy, who liked the idea and expanded it with the best suggestions. The book is better for your input.

To Barbara, who has always been the most positive

and supportive friend anyone could have. When she found out she was pregnant, she said to me, "Get pregnant," and not wanting to be outdone, I did. You're the greatest.

To Kelly, who has been my soulmate for close to thirty years now. I don't know what I would ever do without your support on a daily basis. You are so precious to me.

To my many friends who gave me support when I needed it desperately: Judy, Pam, Judith, Jomarie, Lee, Brenda, Frank, and so many others. What would I do without you?

To my family: Mom, Dad, Mike, Julie, Catherine, and the cousins, who let me know that they love me, no matter what. To Paul, who always makes me feel loved, who told me I could do this and helped me to do it. And to Elizabeth, who was denied a lot of mommy-hours so I could get this done. My thanks.

Finally, to the doctors, psychologists, educators, siblings, fathers, and mothers who opened themselves up to me and gave me extraordinary information. I could never have made up the incredible quotes you gave me. Thank you.

Contents

Contents

Preface

"Children are the anchors that hold a mother to life."
                                                    —Sophocles

Our daughter Elizabeth was born when I was thirty-nine-and-a-half years old. She was the realization of a dream. I had wanted to have a child for almost twenty years and shed many tears fearing she would never come. Unlike some women, I did not postpone motherhood in pursuit of some other goal. Alas, the right man did not cross my path until I was thirty-one years old, and we didn't marry until I was thirty-three. Paul was a divorced father of three children. During our courtship we discussed having a child of our own. He said he'd like to father again and "do it right this time." He felt strongly that building a career and supporting a family had interfered with his ability to parent as fully as he would have liked. With this wonderful assurance, we became engaged.

Unfortunately, during our engagement, tragedy struck. Paul's eldest child, his only son, was killed in an accident. Though neither of us was aware of the full impact this tragedy would have on us, we went forward with our wedding plans. Afterwards we came face to face with a new reality. I still wanted to have a baby, but Paul was terrified of the thought. It was a horrible predicament for both of us, and each of us felt badly for the other. We couldn't settle the issue, and we finally separated. After six painful weeks and some therapy, Paul came back home and said, "Okay." It should have been a joyous moment, but I knew how frightened Paul was and what an incredible gift I was getting.

We gingerly moved forward, and after six months of nothing happening and lots of small tests, I went in for my first surgery. It was a small, exploratory one—a laparos- copy, an overnight procedure. They discovered that my tubes were blocked and there were some cysts in my uterus, both common in women my age. If I wanted to get pregnant, major surgery would be required and the optimum time for conception would be in the first few months after it. I had the surgery, a myomectomy.

Meanwhile, the unexpected happened. A television pilot I had shot had been sold. After twenty years in show business as an actress, another dream of mine was being realized. I had a series! The character I played was a divorced mother. That meant I couldn't be pregnant for the first season. If the show was a hit, I knew they could find a way around the pregnancy in the following season. It would take six months for the fate of the show to be determined. So we gambled and waited. Either way I felt I would win. If the show was a hit, I'd just have my baby a year later. If the show flopped, I'd be able to get pregnant right away. Alas, the show only lasted the first season, but it was six months after the surgery when we started trying to conceive. We had let the optimum time for a pregnancy slip by.

The six months we had waited turned out to be crucial, because by the time we started trying my tubes had closed, requiring the doctors to, in essence, blow them out again—a painful procedure. Six months later I was pregnant. Unfortunately, at three months I miscarried. After twenty years of birth control my poor body must have been in shock. ("You want me to go through with this?!")

My doctor told me miscarriages are common in older

women who have not been pregnant before or who had abortions and not to get discouraged—at least I knew I could get pregnant. It took nine long months before I conceived again. Each time my period was late I was ecstatic, then when my period began I would sink into a horrible depression. Ask any woman trying unsuccessfully to get pregnant: it's month after month of painful failures.

When I finally did get pregnant again, rather than feeling fearful that I would repeat the miscarriage, I was strangely calm. I think that was because I conceived on the anniversary of Paul's son's death. We both felt strongly that his son, Michael, was helping this time, and in some strange way it comforted Paul. He felt there was a link between these two children of his.

The pregnancy was true bliss for me despite the fact that I was nauseous the entire time. I have never been happier in my life. I felt centered and on my right path. The joy of feeling our baby move inside me was greater than any I'd ever known. I was finally fulfilling my lifelong dream. Life was glorious.

Because of my prior surgery, I was scheduled to have a cesarean section. So, according to hospital schedules rather than nature, Elizabeth was born on October 24, 1985, at 8:19 A.M. She weighed five pounds, five ounces—small, but perfect. I asked Paul in the delivery room how he felt about the baby being a girl, wondering if he secretly wanted to have a boy. He said, "I'm thrilled. I don't have to do Little League!"

Luckily for me, my mother had flown out to help me with the baby, because once the baby was born I felt as though I was running a marathon. For three months Elizabeth nursed every hour and a half and was awake and crying almost the entire night. This was not how I had pictured motherhood. I was shocked that an experience I so desperately craved was so frustrating. So I did what I usually do: I went to the bookstore to search for some help.

What I found at the bookstore was depressing. All the books I picked up seemed to be talking to the "young" mother. I was a *new* mother, but I was far from young. While many books were excellent and sometimes even helpful, there seemed to be a gap that only the *older* mothers I was talking to seemed to fill. I sensed immediately that we were a different breed. We seemed to be especially conscious parents who came to parenting desirous of doing an excellent job. I began to harbor a secret suspicion that our dedication may even make us better parents. I wanted to find out for certain, so I began this book. I found that late mothers from all over America were willing to open themselves up to me and allow me to explore their parenting experiences. They too felt we were different, and they were eager to talk about it.

Writing this book has been a labor of love and passion. Next to my family, it's the most enjoyable thing I've ever experienced. If you are younger than thirty-five and contemplating motherhood, I hope this book helps you decide what's right for you and informs you how late motherhood may affect you. If you are deciding whether to have a baby and want to know what it may be like, I hope this book gives you valuable information. I trust the input from doctors, educators, therapists, siblings, and husbands will broaden your understanding. If you've decided to have a baby and are about to try, I hope the medical chapters make your pregnancy healthier. If along the way you discover that pregnancy is not achievable, I hope the experiences of those who chose adoption is enlightening. And if you are like me and simply want to know that you are not alone, I hope this book fills some of that gap. Ultimately I hope you come away from having met all these late mothers more enlightened.

Introduction

This book was born out of the recognition of a new phenomenon—the older mother. A previously unusual occurrence, these ranks are swelling, literally and figuratively. Between 1980 and 1990 there was an increase of more than 74 percent in the number of births in the thirty- to forty-four-year-old age category. And from 1980 to 1989 alone there was a 92 percent increase in the number of births to women over forty years of age. These figures reflect what we've all witnessed and can be attributed to two things: postponed motherhood and improved medical techniques for both mother *and* child.

What has caused this sudden phenomenon? And more interestingly, how are these older mothers coping?

What do these women have to bring to this time-honored profession that reflects their mid-life maturity? How are these parents affecting the various child-associated professions? How are their particular needs affecting educational institutions? How is the medical profession addressing their demands? Most importantly, how *does* mothering at age forty differ from mothering at, say, age twenty-five? And what does the future hold for both the older mother and her child?

In 1976 only 28 percent of the women giving birth were in the work force. In 1990, 59 percent of the women giving birth were working, and those numbers are undoubtedly growing. Curiously enough, of the over thirty-five crowd, some say that many were opting either to stay home full-time or were working on a part-time basis only—choosing, it seems, to devote themselves to motherhood with the same energy they used in developing careers. Are these women the "Super Moms" of the '90s?

Motherhood over thirty-five is unique in that we bring to this new "career" fifteen to twenty more years of life experience, wrinkles, and maturity than our younger counterparts. Lest we forget, this age group is that of the high-achieving, well-educated baby-boomers. We achieved things. We got B.A.s, M.A.s, Ph.D.s and sometimes made V.P. Some of us accepted "Mrs." but many retained our "Ms." We were the first generation who had an open-minded attitude about psychologists and sought them. By and large, we had the benefit of good educations and grew up in "Leave It to Beaver" suburban security. We had fathers who worked and mothers who stayed home. Though the world at large slumbered in the Cold War, we were allowed to enjoy childhoods nestled between the Korean War and the Viet Nam War. But our worlds did a 360-degree turn near the end of the 1960s.

Just as our consciousness was being raised by a newly formed Women's Liberation Movement, the Pill became widely available. We were the generation that was there for opening day of the sexual revolution, reveled in it, then sat sadly by while taps was played during the dawning of the AIDS crisis. If we were Americans we grew up with Eisenhower, grieved for Kennedy and King, and saw the nation diametrically change its morals, sexuality, and politics, moving from conservative to liberal and back again. If we were Europeans we grew up with postwar reconstruction, changing boundaries, hippies, and a changing sexual standard.

Most of us were raised to be housewives and mothers but were compelled by the notion of "having it all." As adolescents many of us had watched Donna Reed, the perfect mother stereotype on television. She was the strongest role model we had. We reached parenthood only to find Rosanne Arnold's television character as the new zenith of motherhood. How do these over-thiry-five mothers incorporate all the conflicting societal messages we've heard, and how does it affect the kind of mothers they become?

Clearly these over-thirty-five women have chosen motherhood as a new goal. Unfortunately for many women, especially those successful in business used to simply setting a goal and achieving it, "having it all" just wasn't possible. Biology had to be coaxed—or accepted. And so for some, new decisions had to be arrived at. Other options, never before dreamed of, began to be explored—and accepted. Not only personal lives but professional lives as well were re-prioritized. Suddenly promotions became less important than procreation.

And so we became mothers. We went into motherhood with open arms and hearts and what we encountered turned our well-organized lives, careers, relationships, friendships, and marriages upside down. Often what younger mothers bore in stride jostled us. Sometimes where they "chomped at the bit" we knew how to "go with the flow." Sometimes motherhood was wonderful, sometimes it was as awful as feared. Yet regardless of the cost, I don't know one mother who doesn't think this is the most important, remarkable thing she's ever done with her life. We are all dumbstruck and in love with the whole experience. Well, perhaps not the *whole* experience. We're not crazy about never getting a decent night of sleep anymore. And many of us haven't the energy required to deal with the "terrible twos." Whoever said kids keep you young must have been young herself.

Our world is split between many generations. We have parents of retirement age and older (if they are still alive). Many of us have husbands who are older as well. Some of us deal with step-children from our husbands' previous marriages. Side by side on our coffee tables are copies of *Parent Magazine* and *Modern Maturity*. While changing diapers we discover liver spots on our hands and grimace in pain when our toddler grips an arthritic finger. We're entering our children into preschool at the same age our parents saw us graduate from college.

While much of mothering is exactly the same despite one's age, mature mothers' commitments, decisions, and concerns differ vastly from those of younger mothers. Life experiences, career ups and downs, and brushes with death (our own and others') alter our appreciation of the miracle of birth and the importance of child-rearing.

For many women who will read this book, delaying motherhood is an option they still have. I hope this book will serve to enlighten these women as to what the future holds. For those of us who have embarked on the late parenting journey, this book seeks to illuminate. I have spoken to medical experts, siblings, fathers, grandmothers, educators, psychologists, and, most importantly, to many other mature mothers. I have tried to define the uniqueness of the path we have chosen, undertaking parenting at thirty-five-plus, so that we can learn from one another about the good, the bad, and the surprises we have discovered.

Only time will tell if we turned out to be better mothers, but one thing is clear: We are certainly older and hopefully wiser!

Part I

The Medical Side

Chapter 1

Decision Making

"Making the decision to have a child—it's momentous. It is to decide forever to have your heart go walking around outside your body."
—Elizabeth Stone

Nothing is worse than the unknown. My mother always says, "Better the devil you know than the devil you don't know," and I believe it. When a reality is placed before us we have no choice but to accept it and make the best of it. But when it is our responsibility to *make* the decision—ahh, the weight of it all. Because once you *make* a decision you have to *live* with it.

When my mother gave birth to me she said it was not just her young age that accounted for her easy acceptance of motherhood, but the attitude of her generation. In earlier eras children truly went hand in hand with marriage. The majority of married women stayed home and motherhood was their career. Their options were not so much limited as defined. It was *expected* that a wife would become a mother. While we could argue the chauvinism of that thinking, it can not be disputed that this certainly made one aspect of motherhood easier: the decision.

Certainly, no woman in her twenties makes the decision to have a baby without thought. But it is not a decision as fraught with fear and anticipation as the one made by a thirty-five year-old. A woman who has not had a child by age thirty-five has usually spent those extra years building a career. If she's fairly lucky, she has achieved a certain level of success and financial security. It is much different to jeopardize a fifteen-year career than it is to threaten a three-year one. Some people feel, sometimes correctly, that the longer the career, the better the seniority, and sometimes the better the flexibility. That is often the case: job sharing, a relatively new concept, seems to be an invention created by mothers trying to juggle both careers and children. Many women have successfully managed to combine these two needs and come out ahead. However, some cannot see any possible way of making the fusion. Still others are unnerved by the examples they have observed of others. Christine, one mother with whom I talked, said,

> When I was thinking about having my son, all I could think about was all the other women in the office who said they were going to take their maternity leaves and come right back—and then never did. Well, I wasn't in a position to do that. We needed my income. It scared me. Did it mean I wasn't going to be as good a mother as these other women? Besides, I'd go crazy locked up at home all day. I couldn't put together the two

feelings: wanting a baby and to be a good mother to him and also wanting to work. It made me crazy for a while.

The double messages women are getting today are confusing. On the one hand, we think we should be home baking cookies (like Barbara Bush) and on the other we feel obligated to be in the work force (a la Hillary Clinton). For some, this dilemma is doubly hard—we may want to be there to make hot chocolate for our kids when they get home from school, but we also want to nail the deal we've been working on for months. Our husbands don't have it any easier. John, one husband, told me,

I want my child to have the most secure upbringing possible, and I think that means having her parents—both of them—around as much as possible. I think "quality time" is a load of bull. There's no such thing. The quality moment may have taken place at 3:25 when your kid got home from school after a rough day and needed Mom or Dad to talk to. That moment may not survive until 7:30 when the two exhausted parents get home. They may be too wiped to listen. I don't think you should have children if somebody's not prepared to be there for them. I've rearranged my work schedule and so has my wife. Now there's always someone home when she is. I may not be on the fast track to success like I once was, but I sleep better at night, and frankly I think this is more important.

Leaving children with caretakers is not a new phenomenon. In the past, however, the children of working mothers were often left with family members. Today, blue-collar workers suffer the biggest challenges to finding adequate child care. And many white-collar working women turn to them for their child care needs. Housekeeper/nannies, once employed exclusively by the wealthy, are now employed by many working couples. Moreover, many have had to turn to alien labor in order to hire child care help they can afford. So rampant and pervasive is this new practice that in the United States, a President had difficulty filling a cabinet post because of it.

However, leaving a child with another person or a child care facility which is probably new to you may not be easy to do, particularly when that child is young and helpless. Some women have much more trouble than they anticipated when returning to work after childbirth. Decisions that you think you have already made may suddenly demand a second look. Beth, a late mother, said,

> I knew I wanted to go back to work and assumed we'd just get a housekeeper, but once our son arrived I realized it meant entrusting his care to someone else. And since we're not enormously wealthy—in fact far from it—I was going to have to consider someone who barely spoke English and couldn't drive. I couldn't handle that, so I cut my hours back and now I juggle constantly.

Not every woman has trouble bringing help into the home or in finding a reputable child care facility or a conscientious babysitter who perhaps takes in several children. Regardless of the route you choose, there is bound to be some adjustment. A mother who suddenly has her movements restricted will undoubtedly have moments of longing to be free. Conversely, the woman who chooses some form of child care will also have other dilemmas to deal with. Nancy told me,

> I knew we were lucky to have my mother look af-
> ter our daughter, but then Mom and I don't always
> agree on the way she should be handled. I know
> that if I were home with her she'd be getting a dif-
> ferent kind of mothering. But she'd also have a
> mother who wasn't too happy. So I guess it's the
> best possible solution. But it's not without guilt
> feelings sometimes. For example, my mother was
> the first one to see her take her first steps. I missed
> out on that. I also don't think our society is sup-
> portive of working mothers, so that adds to the
> guilt.

Without a doubt, the working mother's (and father's)
major dilemma is in finding child care with which they
are happy and comfortable. It is no easy feat. For a couple
who have waited a long time for this precious commodity
(their child) it is sometimes even more agonizing. And regardless of how wonderful the best care-giver can be,
many women still feel that no one can replace a mother.
There is a Spanish proverb that says, "You cannot pay
someone to do what a mother does for free." So if we
hold our breath when the parking attendant drives off
with our new car, fearing the worst, how much more difficult to leave our own flesh and blood in the care of someone else? Someone who may be an acquaintance at best?
Someone who may even have difficulty communicating
with the emergency operator because they do not speak
our language well enough? Tragically, there are very few
of us who enjoy extended families willing or able to help
out. And with our being older parents, our own parents
are often too elderly to help out, even if they are willing.

And that's why the decision to have a baby is difficult. A woman doesn't know for a fact how she'll react once that baby arrives. For many it is frightening to contemplate even the possibility of saying good-bye to a career that has helped define them for the past fifteen to twenty years.

However, to some women the chance to rethink a career is welcome. After years of battling to stay afloat, get ahead and succeed, the thought of staying home is very appealing. I was one of these women; I couldn't wait for a break. (Luckily my husband supported this decision, literally and figuratively.) Probably because of the way I was raised (i.e., to be a housewife and mother) it was comfortable to "just" be a housewife and mother. And I felt that way until my daughter entered nursery school when she was around three. At that point she was beginning to expand her little life and it was time to rethink mine.

One of the most important aspects to look at when making the decision to have children is the state of your marriage. If a marriage is shaky or a husband and wife can't agree on whether to have a baby, the experts say the best advice is *don't*. They suggest counseling or, if possible, waiting. Babies can be very stressful on a marriage (see Chapter 7). And while for many couples a child binds the marriage, for some the child can cause a gap. Said Jenine, one woman I talked to,

> I think particularly when our daughter was small it was hard on our relationship. I devoted so much of myself to her that my husband felt left out. It's hard finding time for everyone's needs in the family.

The state of one's marriage is crucial at any age, but when you are older it is even more crucial. First, if you are a dual-career couple, there have been financial decisions made that were dependent upon the amount of income you both make. The longer that money has been coming in the more likely your lifestyle will reflect it, and the more dependent you probably are on both those incomes to maintain it. If one salary suddenly stops or is cut significantly, can the family survive? More to the point, do both people agree to whatever decision is made? Is the husband willing to shoulder all the financial responsibility? If a woman wants to stay home and her husband feels both paychecks are needed to pay the mortgage, what do you do? What happens when she really wants to get back to the office and he's deeply concerned about the child being in day care all day? These are emotional issues. It is better if your marriage is in good shape to resolve them.

If a marriage is strong, that poses its own problem. If a woman likes her marriage so much, why change the status quo? This proves particularly difficult for people who, by virtue of being older, are more set in their ways. Said Carol, one wife,

> I loved the life we had. We traveled a lot. Everything was neat and organized. And the strangest thing was that even though I was desperate to have a baby (one surgery, one miscarriage), once I was pregnant I started to mourn the loss of the life my husband and I had. I started to think I was crazy to take this wonderful life and throw it away.

When a baby enters any couple's life, there is a predictable adjustment that has to be made. Yet every first-time mother I interviewed said she had no idea how extensive the adjustment was going to be (see Chapter 6). And while the adjustment is overwhelming in and of itself, it is the profound realization that this adjustment is forever that truly alters you. Jill, one mother, said:

> When my baby was about six months old I remember thinking one day, "Okay guys, you can come and rescue me now. I've been a good sport. I haven't had more than two hours sleep at a time in over six months. I haven't complained. I haven't yelled at anyone. This can end now." And then it hit me. This was it. I was in for the long haul. Even if we got a sitter and went to a movie, I still had to come back and face another night of pacing the floor with a crying baby. I joked that a new form of torture should include caring for a colicky baby, because that's what it was for me—torture. I couldn't believe this creature that I was so desperate for was making me so miserable. Ironically, I was also falling so in love with her that I also understood, deep in my gut, how someone could murder for their child. So it was an interesting time.

Just as we block from memory the pain of childbirth, so also does time enhance the joys and erase the memories of how difficult babyhood is on families, particularly mothers. However, for first-time mothers of all ages, this is a difficult and emotional time. It is no wonder that women have historically banded together. Only one mother can know how truly stressed another mother is. This in no way demeans the father's adjustment. Fathers as well as mothers experience the enormous change a baby brings into a family. Some men must also cope with the seeming abandonment of their wives in favor of the newcomer. Despite this, it is women who most keenly feel the pull of both husband and child. Hence the exhaustion. Mary Ann said,

> I knew I was abandoning my husband, but I was really doing the best I could do. After nursing a baby all day, I wasn't much in the mood for someone else having the use of my body. When I look back on that time, even though there was a lot of joy, there was also a lot of strain between my husband and me. Once the baby wasn't nursing, life (our sex life, that is) could begin again.

There can be no thought of having a child without facing the possibility that you might not have a healthy one. When asked what she wants, every pregnant woman always seems to answer, "A healthy baby." Yet some women aren't so lucky. This truly is the most fearful aspect of the whole decision for an older mother. Gone is the cockiness of youth to push you forward unaware and uncaring about the dangers. Older mothers have read about, understand, and have seen the results of tragic pregnancies. We know our age increases the odds of such tragedies. We just don't want to be one of them. And yet we know getting pregnant may place us in this unenviable position.

We are fortunate to live in this day and age when medical technology gives us so much help and guidance. For prospective older mothers, Chorionic Villi Sampling (CVS), amniocentesis, ultra-sound, and other genetic testing can help in the decision making process. When a pregnant woman is thirty-five years of age or older most doctors strongly recommend testing; when the woman is past forty physicians almost insist on it. While these tests can alert you to literally hundreds of possible defects, not one parent wants to be faced with the possible decision that the results of this test can bring. Abortion, while still an option, is a gut-wrenching experience, especially in the case of a much-wanted child. For some, abortion is no option whatsoever.

The first and greatest lesson we learn when we choose to be a mature parent is that we are now, sometimes for the first time in our lives, vulnerable. In a way it is this vulnerability, more than anything else, that frightens us. Our future is in the hands of the fates. For a generation who has for so long felt in control, this is a tremendous shock. Our parents' generation found out early what has taken us twenty extra years to arrive at. Our lessons are coming belatedly, but we hope to be excellent students.

In my own case, for years I looked at older mothers and saw something I couldn't quite define. It was a steady look in the eye, a sense of solidity in their beings. I now know that manner was born out of becoming a late mother. Each woman risked something far greater than climbing a mountain or jumping out of a plane or making CEO. Her maturity made her aware of the dangers, yet she risked becoming a mother anyway.

It is a painful, personal, frightening decision. There are no easy answers and no guarantees. It takes a kind of courage you've never known before, and when all is said and done and you've decided to go for it, you just jump off and *pray*.

Chapter 2

Before You Get Pregnant

"An ounce of prevention is worth a pound of cure." So says the old adage, and when it comes to pregnancy, nothing could be more true for the older mother.

For years we have all heard the importance of good prenatal care. Doctors continually stress the importance of early medical attention for a woman and her unborn child. This attention to prenatal care has resulted in the improved health of our children. But lately doctors and scientists have been aware that *preconceptional* health may be just as important as prenatal care.

For women whose age already places them in a high-risk category, additional concerns are best addressed even before pregnancy begins. Some doctors call babies being carried by older, first-time moms "premium pregnancies" (though actually any and every pregnancy should be treated as a premium pregnancy). When asked what older women can do to insure a good outcome to their pregnancies, Dr. Lawrence Platt, Chairman of the Department of Obstetrics and Gynecology at Cedars-Sinai Medical Center in Los Angeles and Professor of OB/GYN at UCLA School of Medicine, said, "First and foremost, pre-pregnancy counselling." In other words, if you're even *considering* getting pregnant, the best thing you can do is visit your gynecologist.

Says Dr. Irwin Merkatz, chairman of the Department of Obstetrics and Gynecology at Albert Einstein College of Medicine in New York, "The first pregnancy visit is too late to prepare for pregnancy. The preconception visit may be the single most important one in the course of prenatal care."

Pre-pregnancy care, education, information, and, when necessary, behavioral or lifestyle changes are new to our way of thinking. But the benefits of prevention to both the older mother and infant are phenomenal.

When looked at closely, the suggestions for pre-pregnant woman seem logical and simple, but the costs of not heeding them are major. Most women don't know for certain that they are pregnant until they are weeks into their pregnancy. By then it is too late to make these adjustments and the consequences of not having made certain changes are in some cases quite serious, in others, fatal. Here are some examples of areas where preconceptional care can be helpful:

Screening for Rubella: If you have not been vaccinated beforehand, it is too late to do so once you have conceived. German measles is a highly contagious disease. If you are exposed during your pregnancy, the results can be disastrous. Many doctors even recommend aborting during the first trimester. Babies can be born deaf and/or blind, among other things.

Medications: Certain medications have been found to be extremely risky while pregnant. Preconception counseling gives the patient time to readjust to a safer medication for the duration of the pregnancy. Quite often there are other medications available that serve you but are not harmful to a developing fetus.

Drugs: Use of recreational drugs and alcohol are known dangers to the fetus. The tobacco and alcohol industries now admit their danger to unborn infants. Likewise, restaurants must display warnings citing the dangers of alcohol and smoke to individuals. Addressing these issues and informing the patient of the actual damage these drugs produce gives the patient time to readjust her lifestyle.

Nutritional Counseling: In the United States, nutrition is unfortunately often looked upon as something for health addicts. While we talk a great deal about it in commercials, privately we have a generation of women who quietly starve themselves. Though this is not a healthy practice for anyone, we must not forget that developing embryos and fetuses are wholly dependent upon the diet with which a pregnant woman supplies them. During pregnancy, the food that is taken into your body is crucial to supporting a healthy baby. Your doctor or a nutritionist can give you the necessary guidelines.

Environmental Conditions: Whether at home or in the workplace, counseling can alert a woman about potential hazards. Most women have little to fear, but if the workplace proves hazardous, pre-pregnancy counseling at least gives a woman time to rethink career options and, if necessary, allows time for retraining in a safer job.

Genetic Counseling: Doctors can help evaluate a patient's likelihood for certain inherited disorders. In some families there may be a history of Tay-Sachs disease, sickle cell anemia, cystic fibrosis, muscular dystrophy, or hemophilia, among others. With counseling, doctors can evaluate your likelihood for these or other inherited diseases. This provides a woman with the information needed to make personal choices regarding her pregnancy.

Infections: It is not unusual for a woman to harbor an unsuspected infection in her body. If an infection is not causing any major symptoms, it can go undetected for quite a while. Under normal circumstances this would be a problem, but once conception takes place, this could create a difficulty when it comes to treatment. As an example, chlamydia, a common infection, would be best treated with tetracycline. But this is one of the antibiotics not recommended for pregnant women due to possible side effects to the baby. A pre-pregnancy test would determine if any infections were present and treatment could occur before any pregnancy began.

HIV Testing: Testing for the HIV virus before pregnancy is advised for all women. A baby born with AIDS, doomed to die prematurely and in pain, is a tragedy. If a woman is a carrier of the HIV virus, she hopefully would not willingly go forward with plans to become pregnant once her condition is revealed.

Fathers-to-Be: Not only are mothers-to-be in need of a pre-pregnancy medical review, but the fathers' health and medical history needs to be examined as well.

One of the first companies to aid women planning to become pregnant and assess their risks is Perinatal Health, Inc. of Citrus Heights, California (800-562-4456). Perinatal Health has a questionnaire known simply as *Before Pregnancy.*

Patients are asked to fill out a seven-page health inventory. Various topics covered are medical history, reproductive history, infectious disease history, medication history, social and occupational history, nutritional history, and family history. When completed, the form is mailed to Perinatal Health for evaluation. Results can be received either directly or through your physician. The profile, or Pregnancy Planning Guide, consists of approximately twenty to twenty-four pages of detailed, personalized educational information. The amount of information will vary depending on the patient's history.

So impressive is this kind of medical help that many insurance companies now offer this service with their coverage. Whether or not your insurance company covers the cost of a pre-pregnancy workup, for the older mother, this kind of service is well worth the added edge it gives her in achieving a successful pregnancy.

Chapter 3

Facing Infertility

If television star Roseanne Arnold can talk to a magazine like *TV Guide* about consulting fertility experts and news reporter Connie Chung can announce that she and husband Maury Povich are trying desperately to have a baby to *People* Magazine, then infertility is definitely out of the closet. Once mistakenly thought to be a virility problem, infertility problems that were *never* talked about twenty years ago now are frankly discussed on television and radio talk shows.

Celebrities, however, have an advantage that most couples (or single women) don't usually have. That is large financial resources. Attempting to cure infertility often places a couple on a merry-go-round. It is an expensive ride, and not everyone can afford it. Insurance companies often disallow infertility treatments, claiming they are elective procedures and not necessary, which means couples choosing to take the gamble (take home baby rates are low) make not only an emotional commitment, but a substantial financial one as well. Couples would do well to check with their insurance company for a list of what procedures are allowable and then check their savings.

So enormous is the growth in this industry that in the United States a consumer advocacy group has emerged. It is called RESOLVE, and operates out of Somerville, Massachusetts. RESOLVE (their helpline number is 617-623-0744) provides not only fact sheets but also a physician referral service with over eight hundred carefully screened doctors in the United States and Canada. RESOLVE's mission also includes increasing the visibility of infertility issues with insurance advocacy and public education. On a local level, they have support groups operated by fifty-seven chapters around the country. Their knowledge may be useful to anyone caught in the infertility labyrinth. They are striving to be a voice for infertile couples as well as an information source. The group now has support chapters based in most U.S. cities. According to RESOLVE's research, 4.9 million people in the United States are affected by infertility, which is 8.5 percent of couples in their childbearing years. RESOLVE states that infertility is a medical problem wherein approximately 40 percent of infertility is considered due to a female factor and 40 percent due to a male factor. In the balance of cases the resulting infertility may be caused by problems in both partners or cannot be explained.

Statistics and numbers are cold comfort, however, to couples who long to parent. It is not that infertility is new,

Chapter 3

it's that the growing number of older women wishing to produce their first child is. One doctor expressed a view that is shared by many,

> It's not that women in the 1950s who were thirty-five didn't have babies. But I'll bet you most of those babies were surprises. Whereas the thirty-five-plus-aged women now are *choosing* to have these kids. They're really *wanted* babies.

Wanting a baby and being able to have a baby are two different things, especially for older women. So ingrained in our thinking is the assumption that to parent is natural that we believe becoming pregnant is simply a matter of choosing when. This assumption is based on years spent avoiding, rather than preparing for, the event.

When a girl begins menstruating it is often accompanied by the necessary discussion of the new responsibilities of being a woman. I remember being awed by the new capability of my body to prepare a place for a baby. From the time of her first menses a female is reminded by nature of its possibilities—each and every month.

When a young woman becomes sexually active she usually takes the next step in accepting these new responsibilities. She becomes versed in birth control methods. Thus we actively interfere with nature in order to prevent any unwanted pregnancies. We fret over birth control methods. We panic over late periods. We wage a battle with our bodies so that we don't find ourselves pregnant. Then the day comes for many women whose biological clock is ticking when a yearning takes hold for a child. It is at this point the decision is made to have a baby and the body balks.

Women in their forties who are now trying to get

21

pregnant lived through the sexual revolution of the 1970s. The Pill with its high success rate gave us the answer to our mothers' worries about "getting pregnant." And there went the old argument as to why we shouldn't be engaging in "free love," as it was called. AIDS was twenty-five years away. A host of sexually transmitted diseases (gonorrhea, syphilis, etc.) were treatable with antibiotics. Our mothers' cases for sexual abstinence were growing weaker. And what we didn't talk about with them was the fact that if a woman did wind up pregnant, there was the option of abortion. As women, we felt liberated and finally able to express our sexual desires with the same intensity that our male counterparts had been enjoying all along.

What our mothers didn't foresee but perhaps instinctively knew was that in changing women's life patterns there would be some fallout—a day of reckoning. One example of this has been the growing incidence of endometriosis. But because these same women went on to be busy career women, they often ignored the pain they were experiencing in their uteruses. Says Dr. Randy Harris, an expert in endometriosis,

> A lot of women put off treatment for endometriosis because no one has talked to them about the results of *not* getting it treated. Most women don't even know what to look for. They don't realize that if they get treated early they could be increasing their chances of having a baby.

Endometriosis has been called a career woman's disease. It is one of the major causes of infertility in women today. While being dedicated to stimulating, self-affirming careers has been essential and rewarding for many women, few realized the price they inadvertently would wind up paying for those careers. Unlike men, women's equality does not include being able to parent at any age or stage of life. Very few women even contemplated what great sacrifice the postponement of motherhood would be. Many ask in utter disbelief, "What do you mean, I can't have children?" Weren't we lead to believe we could have it all? That all it took was hard work and dedication? Small wonder many women faced with infertility are having major emotional problems—this was something for which no one prepared.

However, mature women who discovered they wanted to be mothers weren't the only ones facing difficulty getting pregnant late in life. Because of the extremely high rate of divorce in this country (50 percent of all marriages end in divorce), later remarriages have made people who thought they were through with having children rethink their decision. Francine, one such woman whom I interviewed, described it this way,

> I was forty-two when I remarried. I had no idea I'd be thinking about having another child at this stage of my life. My daughter (from a previous marriage) was about twelve. I thought I was done. Little did I know.

In the past twenty years, the number of women seeking infertility treatment has zoomed up. Those doctors who trail-blazed this new frontier years ago had no idea how enormous their field of specialization would become. Nor did they have any idea how many couples would benefit from these new procedures.

Says Dr. Richard Marrs, considered one of the country's leading specialists in infertility,

> I started doing infertility work around 1978 and I

can't tell you how many people thought I was crazy. A doctor I was working under at the time said to me, "You know, if this [infertility research] fails, you've blown your whole career." But I had been frustrated by not being able to help more of the women I'd been working with with microsurgery. I wanted to do more.

Luckily Dr. Marrs forged ahead and in August 1981 delivered the second test-tube baby in the United States. In 1982, when such procedures were first beginning to be done, there was an arbitrary age limit set on women who could qualify for IVF (in-vitro fertilization). According to Dr. Marrs,

> We originally stopped doing IVFs on women past forty, but we've extended that now, because even though the higher a woman's age, the lower her chances, we still have some success. And those women should have a chance to fulfill their dreams. But from the onset you do have to realize that the fecundity rate [ability to produce] drops rapidly when a woman ages. For example, when a woman is thirty-four years old her fecundity rate is 20 percent per cycle. By age forty-four it's 5 percent per cycle. But even if that forty-four-year-old does conceive, the miscarriage rate goes up. Her miscarriage rate is about 35 percent. Under thirty-five years of age the miscarriage rate is only 15 percent. And it's not so much a woman's system but the age of her eggs which creates the anomalies.

Dr. Marrs says that over 50 percent of his patients are

over forty years of age. When asked what the procedure is when a couple comes in, he explained that his first consultation with a patient consists of a review of the available options, with input about the success rate for each procedure given a patients age and physical situation. He then asks the patient to think over the options, come back with any questions and then proceed with whatever choice the wife and husband have made.

But many couples who seek out Dr. Marrs (and probably most other infertility specialists) come loaded with a lot of psychological baggage. Often they have been in and out of doctors' offices, faced years of disappointments (not to mention a mountain of undeductable medical bills), and still don't have their much desired baby. Because of their emotional vulnerability, many couples are taken advantage of. Couples need to be careful. Dr. Marrs observes,

> These couples have to separate their hearts and minds and make sure the desire to have a baby isn't going to drive them into a wall. Most of the women I see have postponed getting pregnant almost universally because of their careers. They never thought they *couldn't* get pregnant. They're flabbergasted because they could achieve everything else they set out for and they're stunned they can't do this. These women, often super-achiever types think, "If I just try harder, longer, I can do it." And many times they can't. Some of these couples, who've been having six, seven, nine years of mechanical sex in order to get pregnant often wind up divorcing because they can't achieve what they want.

The cost of infertility is not only emotionally high but financially high, too. All the doctors interviewed suggested caution when looking for a specialist. You don't want to be taken advantage of when you're in such a vulnerable state. It is an expensive procedure. Dr. Marrs states that at this time the average cost for IVF in the United States is at the very least $7000. GIFT (which involves injecting one or more eggs mixed with washed sperm directly into the fallopian tubes with the hope that fertility will occur inside the woman) is around $500 more and egg donations another $2500. When a woman has no womb and the decision is made to go to a surrogate, costs can go up to $35,000, plus $6,000 to $8,000 per cycle for medical costs.

One of the most successful new procedures (egg donations) involves treating the patient with hormones, harvesting eggs from a young donor, mixing them with the husband's sperm and placing it in the wife's womb. This child then becomes the woman's *biological* child, though not her *genetic* child. The appeal of this method is that there are no legal procedures after birth. Although not the genetic parent, the mother has the joy of knowing she has carried the baby and the father has a child who has a biological connection to him. This is particularly appealing to many couples who, for whatever reason, reject adoption.

Some couples do adopt and, curiously, a major reason can be that the idea of using donated sperm is rejected by men in over 60 percent of cases. Says Dr. Marrs, "The men want to go *straight* to adoption, whereas a woman will say, 'Hey, give me a plastic egg, I don't care. It's my baby!'"

Once an older woman has achieved a pregnancy there is a greater risk of miscarriage, especially during the first trimester. The reason doctors encourage women over thirty-five to have prenatal testing is due to the great rise in chromosomal abnormalities due to increased age (from 1 in 700 at age twenty-nine to 1 in 80 at thirty-nine to 1 in 8 at age forty-nine). Testing is usually limited to Chorionic Villi Sampling (commonly referred to as CVS), amniocentesis, or ultrasound. In most pregnancies, it is a combination of two—ultrasound and CVS or ultrasound and an amnio.

According to Dr. Lawrence Platt, Chairman of Obstetrics and Gynecology at Cedars-Sinai Medical Center,

> Ultrasound is the window to the fetus. Through it we can perform fetal physical examinations. And while it may not be perfect, it is without a doubt one of the greatest advancements in obstetrics in the past two decades.

Many pregnant older mothers with whom I talked reported having more than one ultrasound during their pregnancies. To date, these tests are considered harmless and are painless. So while the doctor is gaining important information about your baby, you are allowed to see what stage of growth your baby is in, which is always a bonus for the pregnant mother and father. Unless, of course, the ultrasound reveals unhappy results.

The beauty of CVS sampling is that it gives you many of the same results as an amniocentesis but can be done much earlier in pregnancy (generally starting in the ninth week for a CVS as opposed to the sixteenth week for an amniocentesis, though some amnios can be done earlier). CVS testing can also be done by one of two methods. One is transabdominal (with a needle inserted through the abdominal wall) the other is a transcervical (with a small needle inserted through the vagina and cervix). In both methods a small tissue sampling is taken from the developing placenta. CVS testing has received some adverse publicity which may concern some couples. According to Dr. John Williams, Medical Director of the Prenatal Diagnostic Center and a pioneer of CVS testing in the United States,

> CVS testing has gotten an undeserved reputation as being riskier, but it really depends on who's doing the testing. Without question, you need to make sure you have a properly trained staff and all the necessary equipment. Many couples who are connected with health policies such as HMO insurance sometimes have to face a difficult dilemma—have the procedure done by someone who isn't as knowledgeable but whose fees are covered, or go to someone better trained but not covered. It's a problem. I also think that those who are not as well trained are the ones who are giving us the bad press.

Making such traumatic decisions put older couples in a bind. After years of experiencing infertility, they may be financially strapped but emotionally desperate to ensure the safest possible procedure for a pregnancy.

The most common method of amniocentesis today is transabdominal. Most women reported little discomfort with this procedure. Personally, I disliked it. I wasn't prepared for the fact that the needle was inserted through a muscle to get to the uterus and, therefore, some pressure had to be applied. I also wasn't thrilled because there I was, seeing my baby for the first time on the screen, and I felt we were possibly jeopardizing her safety. I'd be much happier doing the CVS transcervically, I think. But, cautioned Dr. Williams,

> In most cases we can do CVS transcervically. It's quick as well as easy. But sometimes because of the physical placement of the baby or the mother's physiology we may have to go transabdominally.

Sometimes the results of these tests are not what a woman wants to hear. This is particularly sad in the case of a much-waited-for child. Dr. Williams continued,

> It's very hard to have to deliver bad results to these patients. The average age of my patients is about thirty-eight, so for them it's particularly hard. Many women come in who have tested positive on a pregnancy test, and we discover that in about 15 percent of the cases they have a non-viable pregnancy. Either the sack is empty or there is no heartbeat. Sometimes the embryo can be dead six or eight weeks, and when we do an ultrasound we discover that the embryo did not develop.

The pain of being unable to deliver a much-wanted child alive and healthy is profound. It is not something one simply "gets over," for there are constant reminders of being childless. Babies are everywhere. Friends are always having them. They show up at family gatherings. People send Christmas cards with photos of their families on them, and insensitive strangers are always asking, "Why don't you have kids of your own, you're so good with them?"

While nothing can eradicate the pain, RESOLVE, the national consumer organization mentioned earlier, can be an informed and compassionate source of help.

Education, information, and support are vital when one is facing such an emotionally difficult issue as infertility. Without a doubt, the best help always comes from someone who's been there—someone who knows the pain you're going through and who can perhaps help you face your future. You may find that person either through a support group such as one that RESOLVE organizes, through therapy, or with a friend who's shared the same experience.

At some point, the decision you once made about trying to become pregnant is answered either by success or failure. Sometimes we get lucky, and sadly sometimes the answer is not the one we wanted to hear.

Chapter 4

Choosing Adoption

It is no surprise that in this country the vast majority of today's adoptions are age-related. Usually, although not always, adoption is the result of some kind of infertility on
the part of the adopting parents. And those who have
come to the end of their biological road are generally well
past age thirty-five. In the past, thirty-five was considered
the cutoff age for couples wising to adopt, and single
adoption was not an option. Nowadays those barriers are
finally breaking down and more people are being allowed
to fulfill their parenting dreams via adoption. While it may
not be the first choice for a couple or a single person, in
some cases it may be the last, and it deserves a good
look.

For most of us, questioning an adoptive parent seems too personal a thing to do, the questions too probing, the answers too intimate. But if you are over thirty-five it is helpful to look at all the options available to you. The adoptive parents interviewed for this book were generous in sharing their feelings, thoughts, and experiences about the road they are traveling, and they seem to be enjoying the journey.

Birthing an adopted child is often more arduous than any labor a biological mother has seen. Watching friends go through the process has been at times heartbreaking and inspiring, at times enlightening and emotional.

The fates decreed that I was to be the biological mother of my child and that I would be able to raise her myself. But I was fully prepared to give that maternal love to any child I could call my own. When the need to mother is intense ("It was driving me," said Gena, one adoptive mother), you realize that mothering is not about giving birth. It's about raising a child.

The roads that lead couples and single people to adoption are as varied as the roads that lead to any birth. "It becomes a process," said Bunny. "You start out not quite believing what's happening, and before you know it you're committed and anxious to get on with it." Adoption may not be the way one imagined one would become a mother.

> It was so foreign at first. I couldn't believe I was even considering it. I'd always thought I would just grow up and one day get married and have a couple of kids. It didn't happen that way, and it really felt strange to be considering adopting.

For some women pregnancy was attained but never

sustained. Lana explained:

> We lost a baby late into a pregnancy. I really enjoyed being pregnant, but I know now that being pregnant has nothing to do with being a mom. Just because someone has a child vaginally, it doesn't prepare her any more than I was prepared for being a mother. After being there for our son's birth, all I could think was, "Oh God, I am definitely doing this the right way."

Recovery and reconciliation are often part of the process that needs to happen before one can contemplate adoption. Becoming pregnant once (or more) gives one the hope that one can have a biological child. It is only after repeated failures that one gradually begins to think of it not happening. Making peace with that reality is often painful. It takes time to grieve the loss of never having your biological child. Many of the mothers I interviewed chose to deal with the grief in therapy. Some felt that by closing that door, another could be opened. But the decision to adopt usually does not happen overnight. The idea needs time to be accepted and internalized. Said Stacy, one mother:

> I met with an adoptive mom when I first started thinking about adopting, and I liked what I saw. I had gone a little skeptically, but it all was so happy, so natural. So I went to see a lawyer to talk about it. He cost me $600 at the time, and I know it's more now. And that was just the cost of the consultation visit. It didn't apply to the cost of the adoption. So I didn't feel like I could do a lot of comparison shopping, if you know what I mean.

After that first visit, I went away for a few months to think about it. I spent some time in therapy dealing with it, too—grieving, really, over the fact that I wasn't going to be having a biological child. But the more I thought about it, I realized that this was the best way to go.

Sometime the reason a person adopts is not due to infertility. Says Cynthia, a single adoptive mother:

I wasn't adopting because of a biological problem —I'd been pregnant in my twenties and had an abortion—but I was adopting for situational reasons. I didn't have a partner. I had just ended a relationship that had been strained by my desire to have a child. I had thought about going to a sperm bank, but it felt too cold, too scientific. And on a practical level, I knew that I would be out of the job market for six months, sitting at home, gestating this child and going through all the emotional and hormonal changes all alone. It just seemed too sad for me. It had nothing to do with all these altruistic reasons people credit me with. It had to do with an emotional reality that it would just be too sad to be doing it alone.

Irene, another woman who sought an adoptive child, said marrying later in life was why she had waited so long to have a child. When asked why she adopted she said:

We didn't get our daughter until I was forty-three. Although I knew I could become pregnant, I wasn't *getting* pregnant. I knew many friends who had gone through all kinds of extensive tests and fertility procedures. I'd watched their highs and lows, and I really didn't want to do that. Also, my husband was very interested in adopting. My doctor was not very encouraging about my chances of producing a baby, even with fertility work, so I was in a kind of a bind: either get on with the adoption process before we were ineligible because of our age, or pursue extensive fertility testing and work that may never have produced a child. At my age and with the knowledge of all the pain and anguish of fertility treatment, I felt adoption might be the better alternative. Again, if I was younger, maybe I would have pursued biological parenting. But if I'd done that, our daughter wouldn't have been a part of my life, and that would have been a great tragedy.

Every adoptive parent I interviewed felt a destiny and bond with their child and a deep appreciation for the specialness of their child. Said Margaret, a single adoptive mother:

I was all set to adopt another woman's baby. We had agreed months earlier. I had been sending her money. There were regular phone calls. She was set to come out two weeks before the baby was due. We even talked the day before she was to fly out. I went to the airport to meet her, but she didn't get off the plane. I was all alone at the airport. I couldn't believe it. Not surprisingly, she never called again and never answered her phone. I had lost $8,000, but more importantly I had lost my baby. I was so upset I just went to bed. Within forty-eight hours the lawyer called and said,

"Something's just come up. there's a birth mother whose situation just fell through. Do you want to meet her?" I was so upset and confused I didn't know what to do. He told me there would be no time for a regular introduction. I'd have to fly out and meet her, and if we liked each other she would have to fly back with me—which is exactly what happened. Meeting her was the scariest blind date of my life.

The night my daughter was born the lawyer came to visit me in the hospital where I was giving her her first feeding, and he said, "Well, we thought that other baby was meant to be your child, but I guess it wasn't. *Here's* the child that was meant to be yours." And I know he's right. The first time I looked in her eyes, she looked me right back and I said, "Sweetheart, I'm gonna be your mommy, and we're gonna do this thing together," And we are.

All the mothers I interviewed stated that they knew they wouldn't mother any differently if they had given birth physically to these children. They loved the people their children were, the very essences of them. Said Jacqueline, one mother, "My husband and I could never have produced this child."

All the parents I spoke with had chosen an alternative way to become parents and were happy about it. But their concerns about adoption varied. One mother who had adopted said she'd never do it the same way again:

I became attached to the birth mother, and she became attached to me, but when I'd get off the phone from talking to her about the baby, I didn't feel like I was the mother, and I knew that wasn't good for any of us. So I severed my ties with her. We both had to get on with our lives, and I made the decision for both of us. It was hard. I've never had to distance myself from someone I liked before.

Said Marjory, another mother:

I think what helped all of us and gave us some security—if you can feel any during those first six months, when the mother can still change her mind—was that we paid for her to have some therapy. She had some before the baby was born and then after. That way we felt things were being worked out, and also, we didn't want her to suffer. We felt sorry for her. She was a high school girl who'd just gotten herself in a mess, and we wanted this to be as good as possible for all of us. I think it really worked out well for us. Also, when our son grows up we can let him know we really cared and tried to help his biological mother.

Nancy told me:

It would be better for everybody if the laws were unified across state lines.

Corinne stated:

I wish they would abolish the word *adopted*. I hate it when I pick up the paper and they say, "So-and-so is survived by his *adopted* son," or "So-and-so is seen here with her *adopted* daughter." Why must they make the distinction? What purpose does it serve?

Most of the adoptive parents had joined a support group, which helped them deal with various concerns they had. Many felt these groups offered a great deal of knowledge and support for those entering a possibly difficult arena. There is now a National Adoption Hotline you can call (202-328-8072) as well as groups such as Adoptive Families of America (612-535-4829). They publish a newsletter and can provide you with the names of parent groups and agencies in your area. The U.S. Department of Health and Human Services National Adoptive Information Clearinghouse (202-842-1919) has fact sheets and a directory of agencies, as well as information on all aspects of adoption. RESOLVE (617-623-0744) also provides an informative sheet that explains different types of adoptions and includes a list of adoption resources. If you are considering adoption, these resources will prove to be valuable.

Another concern of the adoptive mothers with whom I spoke was how they would feel toward the birth mother. Happily, all reported having good feelings about the birth mother. Katherine spoke to the sentiments of many:

I have such positive feelings about her biological parents because she's such a wonderful child.

Dora explained:

When I first met with prospective mothers, I knew I had to like them. That became the first thing; the looks, the background all came later. I didn't think I could love a child if I didn't like the mother, and I

Chapter 4

think I was right.

When asked about explaining the adoption to the child, Peggy said:

> Are you kidding? In this day and age when they're getting sperm from an unknown donor, eggs from somebody else, and grandma is doing the gestating? I think explaining adoption is going to be a piece of cake.

Each family chooses the right way for them:

> When our son was close to three, we decided it was time to tell him. He'd been asking a lot of questions about growing in my tummy lately, so we felt he was ready. We took him for a walk on the beach and told him that there were lots of ways to form a family and one of them is through adoption, and that's how we made our family. He said, "Oh" and went running down the beach. We were in tears, but he was fine.

Some people are nonetheless resistant to adopting. Each person has to decide what's right for them, said the mothers whom I interviewed. Some of them have passed on their enthusiasm to others. Kathy told me:

> I am directly responsible for two adoptions, and I can't tell you how special those children are to me. One couple had pretty much decided to go ahead with it, and I just provided the shove. The other couple were very concerned because they were afraid that if the child wasn't biologically

39

theirs, it might be different from them. But I said to them, "But you could have a biological child and it could be very different from you. There are no guarantees."

And she's right. Before I had my child I thought that I would get "My daughter." What I got was Elizabeth: a unique human being whose biological origin I happen to share. But love has nothing to do with biology.

In the end, if you want to love a child, there is probably one for you. It may not be the one you imagined, but no child ever is. That's what makes parenting so special: it's a constant surprise. Being over thirty-five may contribute to some of our difficulties in conceiving a biological child, but by this age we know that sometimes fate's plan is not the one we'd have chosen but the one we were meant to follow. And any child that calls you "Mommy" is the child for you.

Chapter 5

When You're Pregnant

While all pregnant women face increased risks to their health, the older pregnant woman faces even more risks. But many risks, if not most, are preventable or controllable.

We live in a society that has greatly increased its awareness of personal responsibility. We continually expand our knowledge of what things are healthy for us, both physically and mentally. So it was somewhat surprising for me to learn through some leading OB/Gyns that what was really missing in the "pregnancy loop" was adequate prenatal care. I had thought that most educated, middle-class women who conscientiously visit their OB/Gyns would be *fully* aware of those things that would help them sustain a healthy pregnancy. But the more I learned from these doctors, the more I understood how haphazard prenatal care can be. I also realized that many mature women, dedicated to having their babies, were totally uninformed when it came to the seriousness of inadequate prenatal care.

Dr. Calvin Hobel, Director of Maternal Fetal Medicine at Cedars-Sinai Hospital in Los Angeles, is conducting a three-year study for the National Institute of Health. The focus of this study is stress in the workplace and how it affects pregnant women. Dr. Hobel noted the importance that stress plays, especially in pre-term labor. The goal of the study is to see what effect, if any, education and support would have on those women who were identified as high-risk pregnancies. What he has observed is that women who are monitored and educated about what to avoid, what to do, and when to seek help greatly increase their chances for successful outcomes to their pregnancies.

All pregnant women need special care, but the older pregnant women needs to exercise special caution. Here is the primary success factor that is being found in Dr. Hobel's study: *Avoid stress*. Stress can be one of the leading causes of pre-term labor. Women today are under a barrage of various stresses; work is one of them. Also, women still remain the primary caretakers of children even during pregnancy, so if this is not a first-time pregnancy, the mother will be responsible for other children. Housekeeping is another responsibility that men do not share evenly even during their wife's pregnancy. Women also spend some of their energies caring for their husband's needs. All these stresses place a pregnant woman at a higher risk, because very few women are able to reduce their stress levels during pregnancy. Accustomed as we have become to the super-woman role, we really think we *can* do it all. And we can wind up paying a very dear price for not slowing down.

Dr. Hobel relates this sad but true story about a pediatrician who was pregnant.

> We had a doctor come into the hospital recently in pre-term labor. She was twenty-two weeks along. At the time she was admitted her OB was unaware of the history that had led to her winding up in the hospital. What she told us, which she had not shared with her doctor, was this: She had left the hospital after doing her rounds on the previous Friday. She flew to Chicago for a friend's wedding, rented a car, and drove for an hour from the airport to the wedding site. She attended the wedding the next day and then drove back to the airport, flew home, and then went straight to the hospital to see patients. The next day she began cramping and went in to see her OB. She was in pre-term labor.

Tragically, this pediatrician, who is also married to a doctor, lost her baby. It was not because she was actively defying her doctor's orders, it was because she was not as *informed* as she needed to be about how risky certain behaviors can be when you are carrying a child. Those of us who are workaholics don't realize the tremendous and possibly fatal outcome this obsessiveness can have on a pregnancy. Said one doctor, "I recently had a lawyer come in in pre-term labor. The first thing she requested was her fax machine."

For all the advances that modern medicine has made, pre-term labor is unfortunately not one of the areas where medicine has made any substantial progress. Relying on medicine, which we have come to expect to be our savior, is neither wise nor possible.

The following advice is offered by Dr. Hobel to help sustain a viable pregnancy:

1. *Avoid stress.* While a completely stress-free pregnancy may be impossible, adjustments can be made to achieve less stress. *Do less.* This is often tough advice for today's woman to follow. We are used to putting undue stress on ourselves, but that stress takes a hazardous toll on the baby, if not on us.

2. *Have a support system.* Because one's work load doesn't magically disappear when a woman becomes pregnant, one way to help get through much of what lies ahead is to have some help. Your own support system may include your husband, your mother, a friend, a sister, or a neighbor. Remember that while you need *physical* support, you need *emotional* support as well. The need will not disappear but may indeed be even more acute once the baby is born. Make sure you're not alone.

3. *Get proper rest.* It is essential to get as much rest as possible. In Sweden, 50 percent of the women in the work force are on maternity leave by the tenth week of pregnancy. By the twenty-eighth week, 80 percent are on leave at 80 to 90 percent of their salary. In the United States, we have a long way to go to achieve this kind of family support.

To illustrate the rest needed, consider that a pregnant woman who stands for three hours needs to lie down on her side for fifteen minutes. This is to insure that the blood supply to the uterus is adequate. Support hose help prevent the blood from pooling in the veins and may improve circulation to the uterus. However, many women find the look of support hose unappealing. In that case, slacks can always be worn. A proper blood supply to you and your baby is of utmost importance, not how you look.

It's essential to do all you can to make certain you get the rest you need.

4. *Eat properly*. Frequent, small meals are the ideal. They create less stress on your pancreas and therefore decrease the chance of developing diabetes. All the nutrition a pregnant woman takes into her body goes to the baby first. If there is any left over, you get it. If not, you and your body suffer. Illnesses such as diabetes and hypertension are not caused by pregnancy, they are merely *underlying physical pre-dispositions that are unmasked during pregnancy*. These illnesses are controllable and even avoidable.

5. *Consult your doctor early*. Identifying whether or not you are at risk can help reduce major problems during your pregnancy. Being older is already a component of a high-risk pregnancy, but it should not indicate a problem in and of itself.

6. *Consider genetic counseling*. New advances in genetic counseling give you more information and therefore more control over your pregnancy and its outcome. CVS (Chorionic Villi Sampling) testing can now be done between the ninth and twelfth weeks of pregnancy. Amniocentesis is done around the sixteenth week. Both methods offer the mother and father vital information to help them determine the health of the fetus. Some families have histories of genetic anomalies. These tests can determine whether or not your baby is carrying these genes. While neither of these tests can offer you complete assurance of a healthy baby, they provide a parent with some important answers.

7. *Listen and Participate*. Successful pregnancy at a mature age requires the expertise of at least one doctor, possibly more. Hopefully you have chosen someone with whom you feel comfortable. It can only help your

pregnancy to heed his or her advice. Some of the doctors with whom I spoke felt mature women are often so accustomed to making their own decisions that they sometimes have difficulty relinquishing any control over their bodies to anyone else—even their chosen doctor. Said one OB/Gyn,

> These women have to realize that the advice I am giving them is solely for the good of their babies. Sometimes I can tell a patient that she needs bed rest and she'll tell me about an important meeting she has to go to. These women don't realize how much risk they're placing their babies in. They put me in a bind. They forget that my responsibility is to *two* patients—the mother *and* the baby. And my primary responsibility is to the baby.

Often, one of the results of maturity is that we no longer place doctors on pedestals. We're fully aware that they are people, too, and that they can make mistakes. Hence many women of thirty-five and up who are pregnant are reluctant to succumb to a doctor's every instruction. Doctors reported to me that most older women tend to read a great deal on the subject of pregnancy and come to their offices quite knowledgeable on the subject. These doctors feel that knowledge is often helpful, but sometimes a *little* knowledge can be a dangerous thing. At some point, they said, we have to trust in the doctor of our choice and heed his or her advice. In other words, if the doctor says we need bed rest, we probably should go to bed.

8. *Avoid the obvious.* By now most people are aware of the dangers of drugs, alcohol, and tobacco on a fetus. By cutting these things out before and during pregnancy, older women are assured of not only a healthier baby but

a healthier mother to care for the baby.

So-called "premium babies" born to older mothers have gotten that name because they are a rare and precious commodity. Since we "house" these babies until such time when they can exist on their own, it is necessary to take whatever precautions are necessary to make certain our "premiums" come due. By taking these precautions we aid the doctor, but mostly we aid ourselves. For those of us who have waited so long to have a child, the reward of a healthy baby is certainly worth it!

Part II

The Emotional Side

Chapter 6

From Birth through the First Weeks

"Adopt the pace of nature; her secret is patience."
—Ralph Waldo Emerson

Most women have special memories of the birth of their children. Did they immediately feel a great deal of love and wonder? For me, the event was all a kind of a daze. While I longed for the baby, I was terrified of the method my doctors had chosen for finally getting her—namely, surgery. Happily, my husband recorded some of the birth on video. When I look at it I find I now react to the wonder of her birth more than I did when I was involved in the process, but my reaction was mine alone. Every birth experience is different. Here's what some other mothers had to say.

Dana told me,

The first moment I saw him I thought he was truly a miracle. I had gone into the delivery room wanting a girl, but when he was born and I saw him for the first time the love was so intense I wouldn't have cared if he was a puppy!

Said Barbara, another mother,

The first time I saw my daughter I felt tremendous joy and at the same time disbelief. I was also shaking so badly I thought there was something wrong with me.

Karen reported,

I was ecstatic. It was like no other feeling in the world. Total blessedness. Total unity. My husband and I both cried. I felt closer to my husband than I ever had. We had worked so hard (it was a difficult delivery) and here was our son—a beautiful combination of Winston Churchill and Buddha.

Roberta said simply, "I was just glad it was over."

Cicely conveyed,

The first twenty-four hours were overwhelming—the sheer amazement of it all. I *never* imagined the magnitude of this miracle that I was a part of, that another human being had come onto the planet. In a room where there were three (me, my husband, and the doctor), suddenly there were four!

In my case, though I had had an amniocentesis, we chose not to know the sex of the baby. I felt it was scary enough having to go through a surgical procedure to give birth. I wanted something wonderful, unknown, and positive to result. I also felt it was my first real test at mothering—to love whatever child I was given, regardless of gender. When I was first pregnant I was convinced I was having a boy. During the last two weeks of my pregnancy I suddenly started thinking about how sweet it would be to have a little girl, that maybe my mother is right, I *should* have a girl. In the end, wishing and hoping didn't matter. What matters is to love what you get. We were sent a girl, and when the drugs wore off I could feel myself falling madly in love, which was just what I was going to need to get me through the year ahead.

The one thing I learned in interviewing mature mothers is that everyone's experience is unique. Not everyone had a baby that wanted to be nursed every two hours for six months—but mine did. We all want to know what motherhood is going to be like. We fantasize about it, particularly during our pregnancies. Toward the end, when we feel like the Goodyear blimp, can't see our shoes and can't get comfortable; some of us beg for it to be over. We want to get on with it. *"Bring on the baby, I'm ready!* Anything's easier than this," we say. Perhaps it's nature's way of preparing us for what lies ahead. By making us eager to get to the next phase, we are endowed with the energy it takes to get through phase one.

I couldn't wait to have a child, and when I was finally pregnant, my pregnancy was so docile and my mood so relaxed and joyful that I just knew this baby was going to be mellow. Her room was decorated, the diapers and clothes neatly stacked, the house clean, the refrigerator full. I even had a manicure the day before I went in for my planned C-section. How much more tranquil could this child's entrance possibly be? Which just goes to show how unprepared even a forty-year-old woman can be when she tangles with nature.

I've never been athletic. I only learned to swim last year. I never skied or was into mountain climbing or any other physical sport that challenged nature. I respected nature from afar, but I never butted heads with her. I knew she was powerful and had a mind of her own. What I forgot when I was having a baby was that *that* was exactly what I was doing. I was butting heads with Mother Nature—and she was going to win every single round! She not only wins, she calls all the shots. She decides the rules and changes them, on a whim, as the game is played. The game I was engaged in was called Babyhood. And what she taught me was that I could control *me,* but I couldn't control the child I was given. No way. No how.

On my second day of motherhood, a nurse took my temperature and discovered a low-grade fever—something many women experience after a caesarian section. I was nursing Elizabeth, and the nurse took the baby *from my breast* and said that I couldn't see her for twenty-four hours. Far from being the tranquil mother I had imagined I would be, I became hysterical. Sobbing, I called my husband and told him what had happened. Within ten minutes, I had my baby back. Luckily, my husband had gotten my doctor to intercede. When the pediatrician arrived some four hours later, I was still crying my eyes out.

Casey, one mother, calmly told me how three weeks after the birth of her baby she was serving a Thanksgiving dinner and spilled a little gravy on the tablecloth. She said she cried so uncontrollably that she was unable to join her family for Thanksgiving dinner. This from a doctor! I was extremely grateful to her for relating her story. Her willingness to share the truth with me about the parenting road she had traveled meant a lot. Thanks to her I no longer felt guilty and alone. But I still worried. It was not like my body to betray me—I was not someone used to being at the whim of my emotions. These feelings were foreign to me. It was one thing to be pregnant and see and feel the changes that were occurring. Those changes I could handle. Emotional changes after my baby was born was another matter—especially volatile ones. *What is happening to me,* I wondered. Was I merely reacting to the drugs working themselves out of my system, was it the hormones, or was something else going on here? We've all heard about women going through post-partum depression, but I never expected it to happen to me. Surely, I was different. Remembering my naïveté still causes me to laugh. What an ego!

Experience counts for a lot. That's why parents are always yelling at their kids, *"Don't touch that outlet! Stay away from the stove."* We've learned a few things along the way. While some areas of learning are fairly undisputable (such as those mentioned) there are a lot of gray areas in life that are wholly dependent on the players involved in a particular situation. While I had a high-maintenance baby, my best friend, who gave birth to her first child a year after I did, had the baby I had imagined would be mine. He was sweet and easy. He slept. He didn't fuss. He slept. He cooed. He slept. My friend's experience was light years away from mine. She has sweet memories of her child's first year of life, while the word *difficult* is an understatement for my experience. Because I considered myself wise and experienced, I erroneously thought that I was in charge of the situation—all I had to do was plan better, work harder, and all would turn out fine. Alas, all my accumulated knowledge proved fruitless. In the world of mothers I was as newborn as my child. Happily, by interviewing other mothers I now realize I was not alone in my unrealistic preconceptions. The vast majority of older first-time mothers had *big* surprises in store for them—surprises that weighed roughly seven pounds, four ounces.

I asked the late mothers whom I interviewed to describe their feelings during the first months of their babies' lives. Here's an example of what numerous mature mothers reported:

> It was hell. I had a hard time coping with the broken-up nights. I also didn't feel like my body belonged to me but rather to my baby. The late afternoon screaming sessions were the worst, though. I didn't realize how bad it was until I got past that period and looked back on it.

In my own case, before giving birth I had been blissfully unaware of the late afternoon/early evening crying some babies exhibit. In my house we called it the cocktail hour cry. It usually started around 5:00 P.M. When she cried, I sometimes had a glass of wine—it helped.

Elaine, one mother with whom I spoke, reported on the first few months this way:

> I was surviving, not living, for the first three months. I couldn't get over how dramatically my life changed. I had thought the baby would adjust to our lifestyle. I didn't understand that *everyone* had to adapt.

Lauren said:

It was absolute torture. He didn't cry, he screamed. I clearly remember walking him around the dining room table and tears just rolled down the faces of my husband and me. Then I'd have these thoughts: *Why did we have this baby?* Then the guilt would set in. When the other children were born they had colic, too; but by then I knew it wasn't something I'd done and, more importantly, that they weren't going to die.

Gail, a mother who had three children in her twenties and another one at thirty-eight when the older ones were almost grown, recalled,

Adjustments were made. Life carried on. Routines were established and we fell into line. I really don't remember any big adjustments, although I'm sure there were some. It all felt very natural to me.

Unlike Gail's easy adjustment, Alice told me, "I just love the baby, the person he is—but the routine has been so difficult."

Luckily, falling in love with your baby helps smooth over the possibly rough transition some of us have during the first few months of parenting. There is no doubt in my mind that the love I felt for my daughter *totally* compensated for the extreme exhaustion I was also experiencing. The first few months of becoming a late mother is a very emotional time. Without question there is also a hormonal volleyball game going on inside, which exacerbates some women's reactions. Some reactions last only for a few days while some can last longer. Just how severe these post-partum experiences are depends on many factors. Most—if not all—are not under parental control.

Chapter 7

How a Baby Affects Your Marriage

Whether you have a baby after nine months of marriage or nine years, the effect is profound on your relationship. Paul and I had been married six years and had lived together for two before that. Today I can barely remember our life before Elizabeth, yet we were together longer before her than the years since we've had her. However, the delineation between the two lives is so strong as to almost obliterate the first. This is not to say our family life is not satisfying, just very different. Still, I recall that critical time when we had made our decision but were not yet parents, thinking over and over again about how much I loved our life and was terrified about it changing. I didn't have a clue about just how enormous that change would really be.

Generally speaking, people who have children are in love. They like to be together. So much do they love each other that they want to enhance their wonderful relationship by adding to it, so they have a baby. But in order to become a family, the couple must dissolve the old relationship and make way for a new one. As in a corporate takeover, there is a new order replacing what was once familiar, and the name on the building is changed. "The couple" becomes "the family." And just as the employees in a takeover worry about their new roles, so it is with couples: *Are we going to like the way things are run in this new place? What exactly are the benefits? Am I going to have to put in any overtime? Do I get any vacation? Will I like my new boss?*

Among the things I spoke about with mothers was how their relationship had changed once they had had a baby. As you will see, some takeovers go smoothly, some are traumatic, and some are a mixed blessing.

Beverly commented, "I don't know if my marriage is better or worse—it's different." Avis added,

> I didn't recognize the change in our relationship right away. My emphasis in the beginning became the children. Lately though, we've both begun to take days off when the kids are in school and just spend the day doing things *we* like—going to antique stores or to a movie—just the two of us.

And Gail looked at it another way: "We are bonded in a new and marvelous way—even though we have less time alone." Casey also lamented the lack of privacy.

> Our relationship has definitely changed. We don't have time together. If we had a bad relationship it

would be awful. There's always someone around—when he comes home we can't talk at the dinner table because the kids are anxious to tell him about their day. When we go to bed at night it's hard to have sex because there's always a kid in the bed.

Maxine wryly said:

Has our relationship changed? No more than if I'd gone to the hospital and come home with a new husband, 'cause that's sort of what it's like. There's a whole new person you have to learn to deal with on an intimate level.

Ann told me her marriage is better. "That's not to say there aren't strains," she cautions, "but the love and challenges have strengthened and bonded us." Teri also mentioned the give and take of the couple's new role:

We're a family now. Not just a couple. As a result we have to work sometimes at just being a couple —just being the two of us.

Loni beamed,

I believe my marriage is getting stronger. We both wanted to be parents because we like children and we like the whole system—it's very nurturing. We were both clear when we got married that we wanted to create a family together. But we were lucky because we not only wanted to have a family, we'd found the right partner to have a family with. I get such a joy over watching him "ooh and ahh" over the children. It's definitely brought us much closer together.

Betty was less enthusiastic:

I think having the kids put a distance between us. I don't think either of us had the ego strength to balance all these demands. I see that the relationship was done growing and stretching but I think we used to have a much different sort of life. There's no time and energy now for just us.

Tobi confided, "We were ourselves for so long it was a hard adjustment—very, very difficult." But for every trying experience, there is a rewarding outcome. Take Ally, for instance. "We're very close. We spend a lot of time discussing the children." No one summed up the conflict more eloquently than Dawn, when she spoke about becoming a family:

Having our son has cemented us in a way that wouldn't have been possible without him. You take a path together when you have a child. When I had my child what became important to me was family. For me, my husband and child became the center of my life, and because my husband sits in the triangle of our family it made our relationship much, much better. In fact, if I could project the impossible (what life would have been like without a child) I don't know how well our relationship would have held up. Until you have a child you don't come into full maturity because before that you're only looking to fulfill yourself. Once you have a child you learn to give in a way that I was

never willing to give to my husband before. That
giving part of me opened up when I had a child.

Each marriage reacts uniquely to the pressures of a
child, as evidenced by some of these sample reactions. In
addition, the experience of having a child is not lived out
in a vacuum—people move, change jobs, have personal
setbacks, or suffer severe financial losses. All these things
affect a marriage whether or not you have a child. The difference is that as an over-thirty-five-year-old parent, the
losses or changes may be more profound and more un-
settling. Some women reported that their husbands were
undergoing mid-life crisis at the same time they became
parents. A few husbands had lost jobs.

This is not to say that younger parents don't have similar problems. But couples who parent in their twenties are
not going through mid-life crises. While losing a job is always emotionally and financially devastating, it can be
doubly so for a mid-life person who knows that getting a
job at that point will be more difficult, especially at the
salary he or she has become accustomed to. Finding
work in your fifties and sixties (the ages of some of these
fathers) is no easy trick. And if you have just taken on the
responsibility of a new baby, the pressure can be especially rough. It is no wonder that some late mothers report
less than picture-perfect lives now that they have had
children.

When I was pregnant I wanted someone to guarantee
me that we would be delighted with the choice we had
made to have a baby. I was so fearful of letting go of the
comfortable life we had before that I wanted complete
assurance that we were doing the right thing. But I felt the
same way when I was getting married. I wanted to *know*
that we'd never have problems, we'd always be crazy for

each other, and divorce would never even cross my mind. Silly me. Life does not work that way. Growth does not work that way. Since the birth of my baby, my marriage has had good days and bad days. Parenting has good days and bad days. Life has good days and bad days.

So even though it may be somewhat reassuring to read of the wide spectrum of reactions that older mothers may have, no one knows what lies ahead. We all live poised on the brink of the unknown, awaiting the future. I don't think anyone should be afraid to parent simply because no one can tell her what's in store. That would be like not celebrating New Year's Eve because you didn't know what kind of year lay ahead.

Chapter 8

How a Baby Affects Your Sex Life

A very private area of parenting, which rarely gets discussed except between close friends, is an altered sex life. Let's face it; sex requires two people, some time, and some energy. Parents qualify in the first requirement only. The other two requirements are only occasionally achieved. I know there will be a hue and cry from those who protest that their sex life is just as hot as ever. But gauging by my interviews, they are very few and far between. The reality is that couples with young children have a very tough time finding the time and conserving the energy for a romantic rendezvous. It's not that it can't be done, and it's not that it *isn't* done, it's just that it's not done as often as it used to be. And when you add normal aging to the process, the libido seemingly quiets down.

For a generation who spoke openly of sex and who participated actively in the sexual revolution, this has been more than an adjustment. It's practically an identity crisis. Now that our mid-life conservatism has taken over there seems to be no one with whom to discuss our fears and changes. We're all seemingly back in the closet.

But to solicit views about mid-life parenting and not address the issue of what happens in your intimate life after you have a baby would leave out a very important element. If someone is thinking of having a baby, that person naturally wants to know how her sex life will be affected. And if you've had a baby you want to know if anyone else is going through what you're going through. It is pertinent information, but going up to someone at a party and asking, "Say Lois, how's your sex life now that little Jacqueline is here?" somehow just doesn't seem like the right way to get it.

Luckily the mothers I interviewed were generous in opening up about so private an area in their lives. Happily, they all displayed a sense of humor about the subject as well. When asked about their sex lives, the women I interviewed almost universally remarked, "What sex life?" I breathed a sigh of relief as these interviews went on and realized that some of the emotions I had been feeling were normal. The women continued:

We don't have sex that much because there's always someone in bed with us.

During sex I worry about the baby waking up and yelling, "Mama!"

I never have sex without a nightgown on anymore. I'm afraid someone will walk in on us.

I've learned to lock the door.

I don't have any energy for sex, and there's *no* privacy!

These women were echoing my experiences! Some even went beyond them:

It's hard to be as spontaneous as before, but it does spark creativity.

The fact that we have an active and satisfying sex life has certainly pulled us through a lot of really bad times.

There is no doubt about it, being a parent certainly takes some of the spontaneity out of sex—no loud exclamations of passion. No more sex on the kitchen table. When you have kids in the next room, sex has to be more furtive. These days my husband and I make appointments, but we really don't mind. We both know this is a short period in our lives and because we're older and hopefully more mature, it makes our new reality easier to make peace with and to accept the inevitable postponement of things we once didn't have to.

Actually, in my own case sex has been better lately. We made a decision to have quality sex instead of servicing. We decided to make this our goal. Sometimes because of exhaustion, parenting, or business it doesn't work out and we just wind up cuddling. And that's great, too.

I think the combination of working, parenting, and just plain dealing with life slows down the libido and the frequency of sex.

Sex is definitely better now that the kids are older. My only worry now is, "What if the lock doesn't work?"

It's better since we started exercising.

Cecelia defined her sex life as changing by stages:

Our sex life? Well, it's been an evolution. When they're infants and you're up all night, there is no sex life. But now that he's a child it's easier. Sex is so unimportant to me but I know the importance of our connecting.

For me, the first couple years after our daughter was born were, as far as sexuality, a blur. I was one of those mothers who was up all night with a crying baby and while I know my husband and I had sex, I don't remember it. But then, not only sex but *everything* was a blur! It has only been lately that my original interest has begun to revive, and that is because we manage our sex life better.

Whenever possible, we plan our encounters for the times when our daughter is not home. It's not that we don't have sex when she's there, but I'm not as relaxed and often exhausted by the time I climb into bed late at night. All I want to do is sleep. Morning is more conducive to love-making because a good night's sleep has energized me.

In the early years after our daughter Elizabeth was born my desire for sex waned. It was an aspect of parenting I hadn't anticipated. I was well into my forties by the time she was sleeping more at night (not that she actually slept all night, just that it was better), and it took a while before I realized I wasn't as interested as I used to be. At first, I attributed my lack of sexual desire to my fatigue. But when I began to have hot flashes and night sweats, I became suspicious.

Many who become older mothers face menopause and its effects just at the time when they may be running after a two-year-old or nursing their children through the chicken pox or some other childhood disease. While every parent's sex life undergoes some kind of transformation, the changes of mid-life add more physical and emotional stress to older mothers' lives due to the time and energy-consuming elements of taking care of a child.

Menopause is the period of natural cessation of menstruation occurring usually between the ages of forty-five and fifty. This is the same period when late mothers are coping with their babies or early childhood. When the onset of menopause occurs simultaneously with motherhood, it will almost definitely affect a woman's sex life. The fatigue and loss of libido become difficult to decipher among all the other stresses that are placed on our bodies. And if you're up all night with a teething child, your sex life will be affected even more. This makes it even harder to determine what's causing the change in your sex life—the loss of libido, menopause, or the loss of sleep.

Our sex lives are important to all of us. Sex is the most intimate way that we connect with our mates. In addition to adjusting to parenthood and possibly menopause, the fact that our sex lives will take some major readjustments is often difficult to face. But the results of my research and my own experiences have made me conclude that everyday family life, despite its joys and satisfactions, interferes with romance—no doubt about it.

Still, I think I'll make an effort to gain some private time with my husband before our daughter becomes a teenager. While she's at school. Right after I put the clothes in the dryer, take the roast out of the freezer, and turn the sprinklers off in the backyard.

Isn't it romantic?

Chapter 9

Small Adjustments

If anyone had told me that parenthood meant embracing rodents, I'd have bailed out a long time ago. It's not that I have a particular abhorrence of small beasts, but pets (in my mind) are creatures like cats, dogs, and, if absolutely necessary, birds. Little did I know I'd have a child who would possess a mania for mice. Our house is cluttered with a million mice—stuffed, porcelain, plastic, rubber, and real. We even have a mouse cookie jar.

The reason I am sending along this bit of trivia is because one of the interesting things I've learned about parenthood is that you surprise yourself with the things you wind up loving. By looking at life through a child's point of view, things take on new meanings. Heretofore undesired items or outings suddenly become fun. Jackie, one mother whom I interviewed, told her experience:

> This weekend we're going to two soccer games on Saturday, and that night there's a soccer banquet. We've become friendly with the other parents, and it's an enjoyable social life. I don't feel I'm missing out on a lot. We're family oriented, so for us it's fun. Sunday we're taking our daughter and a group of her friends to the Hard Rock Café.

Having a child alters how you spend your time for many years to come. The adjustment between what you used to do on a Sunday (or any day for that matter) as compared to what you now do on a Sunday are sometimes difficult. Said Nicole, another mother:

> When my husband and I were together before our son was born, we used to sleep in on Sundays, get up late, leisurely read the paper, and then go out for brunch. Now we have a child who's up at the crack of dawn, and so are we. I sure miss those old days sometimes.

Adult-type fun is very hard to give up. For a late mother, after years of self-determination and leisure, parenthood is restrictive. The adjustment often takes years, and there are always moments when you miss your former freedom. In the first few years, I think the loss is profound. Almost like someone you really loved—the old you—died. And you did. Adjusting to the new you is rather like looking in the mirror and noticing those new wrinkles. It takes a while to make peace with the changes. And I don't think enough is said, or admitted to, about the enormity of the changes.

But in life there is always balance. While I might not get to do adult-type activities on the weekend, on beautiful spring days I rather enjoy sitting on a bench watching a tee-ball game, or building a sand castle on the beach in the summer. But then, I've come a long way.

Almost everyone I spoke with talked about the affect having children had on friendships. Inevitably, major adjustments have to be made. If your friends are childless, there is usually difficulty in relating to why you're now so unavailable, or why you have to cancel dinner plans at the last minute because you have a sick child. Eve recalls an incident to which any mother can relate:

> I had been looking forward to going to a friend's house for a week. She's a great cook, and we enjoy her friends. The afternoon of the dinner party, our daughter came down with a temperature of 102. It wasn't that the sitter wasn't willing to stay with her; it was that the child needed her mother for comfort. And the bottom line is, that's where I wanted to be, too.

If your friends had children earlier who have now grown up, they seem to have forgotten the constraints young children place on one's social life. So, almost imperceptibly at first, you start to form new friendships with parents of children the same age as your own. Being with other parents of children the same age gives you an immediate bond. Friendships often begin easily because of the shared parental experience. And the kids' activities also provide adults with something enjoyable to do that is not work-related. And older parents seem to relate best to other older parents. Alice told me,

I like the other parents on the tee-ball team, but I seem to seek out the older ones. It's not that I don't like the younger ones, it's just that, I don't know—the older ones seem calmer maybe about the outcome of the game. We relate on a level I can't even explain. It's almost like we're bemused by some of the stuff the younger ones get worked up over.

On the other hand, our age alone is often a concern. Many of us have given serious thought to how our age will affect our child. One father reported,

Whenever I go to Little League games, I'm always checking the parents, seeing if anyone else has grey hair like me.

For the most part, societal prejudice against the older parent has ebbed. Thanks to the vast numbers of older parents who are invading every aspect of the baby kingdom, what was once looked upon as unusual is now commonplace. Statistics reassure us that we are indeed growing by leaps and bounds.

Winning the game is not as important as playing and having a good time. Some older parents, like some older people, have lost the ability to play. Being in the work force and being responsible sometimes gets in the way of doing what we knew instinctively as a child—how to have fun. Teaching a young child to ice-skate might remind you of the pleasure of sports. One father told me,

Even if I don't get in the rink with her, it's fun to just sit and watch her do it. I remember what it's like. I haven't rented any skates, but I'm tempted. I may do it yet.

Young parents would probably not think twice about getting on the ice. Older parents—especially someone with a history of back and neck problems—do. One adjustment in older parenting is accepting the reality that physical restraints may have to be accommodated. Many people argue that kids require so much physical energy that it's not fair to the children if Dad (or Mom) is too old to teach them how to play a particular sport. Dr. Lynn Kessler, a marriage, family, and child counselor, doesn't agree.

> It's not imperative for a child to be taught by his or her own parent. You can often find a teenager on the block whom you can hire to throw the ball. As long as you provide the child with the opportunity to learn—that's the main thing.

Today, competence at various sports is often the norm for older parents. One or both have learned and sometimes mastered a sport and are usually eager to pass the pleasure along to their youngster. If the parent hasn't been active in any sport, they are often anxious to make sure that their child is.

Where I grew up, boys played ball and girls didn't. No one had a pool, and tennis courts at home or even at nearby recreation centers were unheard of. Our appreciation for physical fitness is new, and while it would be wonderful to be your child's teacher in everything, handing the chores over to someone else is not such a bad idea. Fortunately, many older parents have the financial resources to do so. I let someone else give Elizabeth a booster shot, why not let someone else show her how to swing a tennis racket? On the other hand, it was because of my daughter that I actually became more physically active. Watching her learn to swim motivated me to finally learn. I wanted her to see that Mommy's still learning and that if I could try hard at something maybe she could as well. The adjustment here was definitely a bonus for me.

Everyday life takes on new meaning when experienced for the first time with a child. The first time we took Elizabeth to Chucky Cheese (a family restaurant that has pizza and activities for children) the gleam in her eyes, the giggle, and the delight were positively infectious. B.E. (before Elizabeth) I had eaten in some of the best restaurants in the world, but none left me with the joy in my heart that good old Chucky Cheese did that day. It is not that grown-ups don't prefer adult pleasures, it's just that after *years* of eating at fancy restaurants the novelty is gone. One mother with whom I spoke put it very well:

> My company had done a lot of work for Super Bowl Sunday, and as a reward we were given a table for the "Taste of Super Bowl." This was a big fancy dinner where they had flown in some of the best chefs from around the country to prepare a gourmet feast. I looked forward to going, but the day of the event our son came down with the chicken pox and I decided I didn't want to leave him. It wasn't a hard decision for me. I've been to fancy "do's" before, so I didn't feel like I was missing a lot. I don't think I'd have felt the same if I was in my twenties.

If you've only been to Chucky Cheese and never been to Chez Gourmet then you've definitely missed something. On the other hand, if you've eaten a bushel of radicchio in your lifetime, a few pizzas can be fun. A world of adult-only activities limits you. It disconnects you from a big chunk of reality—a reality that's cluttered with butterflies, rocks, birds' eggs, and feathers. We adults no longer seem to notice the beauty of things. Children give you a sense of being grounded, of belonging to the real world—a world of simple but profound joys.

We have had a total of four hamsters run away on us. The clever devils don't miss an opportunity for escape should any opening become available to them. Never having had hamsters, I had to learn along with our child how crafty these little beasts were. They've all been named Sparky. After the first one fled, Elizabeth cried the saddest cry I've ever heard from her. It broke her heart, so naturally we had to get Sparky No. 2. Sparky 2 arrived pregnant, which we didn't discover until she gave birth two hours before we were set to leave on a vacation. After checking with the veterinarian, we found out Sparky and the babies had to come with us, wrapped in a heating pad. Sparky gave birth to eight babies, but by the time we had reached our destination there were only five. A horrified Elizabeth told us Sparky had put the babies in her mouth. "Did she eat them, Mommy?" my anguished child asked. The anguished parent in me wanted to know why I'd ever gotten her a hamster in the first place.

Painful though this episode was for all of us, we learned some important things about nature. All the child psychology experts will tell you how important it is for children to have pets; one of the reasons is because of the simple lessons nature teaches them. But what the child psychology books fail to say is that the lessons are not just for children but for he adults as well. Being late mothers, most of us have experienced death through the loss of someone we've cared about. But seeing nature's cycle through the lives of these little creatures is reassuring. It has made me feel part of the whole and has made me celebrate, with Elizabeth, both sides of the life coin. We've already had to bury Berry (the alliteration sent Elizabeth into a fit of morbid laughter) our bird, as well as three mice. Death no longer seems punitive and birth seems all the more joyous.

Side by side my child and I mourn our losses and delight together in the gifts of life. At an age when death was beginning to look like an unwelcome finish line, I got the chance to make peace with it. We buried the bird and the mice under our orange tree, said a few nice words about what they'd brought into our lives, and felt sadness for our lost friends. The next week we got two new mice. We think one of them is pregnant.

Chapter 10

Growing Adjustments

Ages 3–8

Just as the baby experience differs from family to family, so does the childhood phase. My friend with that perfect, sleeping baby now has a seven-year-old who is the most active creature you've ever met. Their house is one big "project" for him. He shuttles between the various construction sites he has devised around the house, and his mother claims the only time she sees her carpet is around ten o'clock at night, when all the debris is put away. I, on the other hand, have a relatively quiet, generally orderly little girl. She easily conforms to the structure in this family and is receptive to putting things in their proper place. I'm *enjoying* this phase; my friend is surviving. She mentioned seeing someone's new baby. She grew misty-eyed, remembering. I shuddered.

Mothers seem to be divided into two camps: those who love little babies and those who prefer children who can hold a conversation with you. I'm definitely one of the latter kind of mothers. Once the "paraphernalia" phase was over, I was much happier. You know that phase: it includes bottles, diapers, toys, snacks, a change of clothes, a stroller, a car seat, and the ubiquitous diaper bag. They can make all that stuff as "designer" looking as they want, but it's still cumbersome and awkward. I don't know what made me happier, throwing away the last bottle or throwing away the last Huggie. I was delighted to leave babyhood behind.

The remarkable thing about parenthood is that it teaches you flexibility with a capital F. While flexibility can sometimes be hard to learn, occasionally it can encompass a nice surprise. Childhood has been a nice surprise for me, but not without some periodic readjustments. The vigilance that was required during babyhood (a self-imposed vigilance, I admit) has blossomed into a far saner childhood period. The transition came so clearly that it was like walking through a door. I remember the day vividly. Elizabeth and I were driving two hours from home to visit Paul, who was away on business. Our normal car ride usually involved talking, singing, food, tapes, pit-stops for toilet visits. But during this ride Elizabeth played with her toys and, except for an occasional exchange, left me to listen to the radio or just think. It was extraordinary. She occupied *herself* for a full two hours. She was close to turning four years old at the time, and it was the beginning of what I call Phase 2: The Easier Years (to be followed by Phase 3: The Dreaded Teen Years).

Don't let all this sentimental reminiscing fool you. When I say these are the easier years, you have to realize you're hearing it from a woman who considered babyhood her personal Vietnam. Give a starving man a stale crust of bread and he considers it a feast. Give me an uninterrupted shower and I consider it a vacation. Phase 2 is *not* without new adjustments that can present their own demanding set of challenges. Figuring out some of the ways to adjust can be positively boggling in its complexity. The real challenges begin when children begin their grade school experience, and those challenges seem to expand with each successive year.

A few families we know, particularly working families, felt things went smoother when their children were in nursery school. A few had on-site daycare where they worked and enjoyed visiting with their offspring at lunch time. Some had a housekeeper who could clean during school hours and then pick the child up after the three-hour session at school. Others were comfortable dropping the child off at a regular daycare facility and picking them up after work. Involvement with nursery schools or daycare facilities can be kept fairly minimal. Once the child enters grade school, things change. They sucker you in during the first year of kindergarten, but by first grade you realize big changes are in the wind.

Carol told me:

School has been our biggest challenge yet. Preschool was easy because we used it to more or less fit our schedules. If I needed to go out of town on business and could take my husband and son, we'd go and make a mini-vacation out of it. Now that he's in school we can't take him out. We took him away for ten days when he was in the first grade, and when we came back he'd missed the whole explanation on subtraction. We learned the hard way that we can't do that anymore.

It isn't that forty-year-olds can't teach their children simple subtraction, but you'd be surprised how hard some of that beginning work is. Do you remember your short *O* from your long *O?* Do you know how to do math with manipulatives? Do you know how to break down a sentence so that an eight-year-old can understand it? (*Example:* Our class went to the museum. *Our class* is the "who" part. *Went to the museum* is the "telling" part.)

Yes, homework, that dreaded enemy from the past, is back. After a long day at the office, sitting down with your child and sloughing through what seems like endless work is very taxing, particularly when you remember evenings from your previous life. Nighttime before Elizabeth used to be a soothing time of day. No longer. Here's what has to be done in the evening: dinner, dishes, homework, reading with her, and bedtime—all this between 6:00 and 8:30 P.M. Often there is also a phone call or two regarding some arrangement for her activities the next day. If she is asleep by 9:00, I finish what wasn't done beforehand. When I get to bed by 10:00 I'm usually too exhausted to read, which used to be my bedtime luxury.

This past year I discovered carpooling, and I love it. Because of it I only had to pull my act together two mornings a week. But one of the women in the carpool just told me her teenager is getting a car and will be taking her child to school this year. My carpool had to be reformulated, but I got lucky. One of the women in my carpool works and doesn't mind taking the kids in the morning if I'll pick them up in the afternoon. This works well for both of us.

Chapter 10

I loathe making lunches. However, my daughter's school only provides lunch on Wednesdays. This year, four mothers decided to "lunchpool." I was only going to have to make lunch once a week for four kids. This seemed like a major achievement, but guess whose child wouldn't eat the other mothers' lunches? Mine.

Sleepovers are a tricky endeavor that begin when the children are around six years of age. We had two last weekend, and both were busts. One child started crying around 10:30 P.M. and wanted to go home. Another made it to midnight. Both fathers were a bit unhappy to have to get out of bed and retrieve their little darlings. But what can you do? Separation is only occasionally successful with a young child. When you hear their little voices on the other end of the phone saying, "Mommy, I miss you. I want to come home," what can you do but throw on some clothes and return your child to their safe port, home?

My daughter is a Brownie. For a child to be accepted into a troop, a parent must be willing to lend a hand. Those services required about three hours a month on my part, plus carpooling the kids from the school to the meetings every other week. Selling the cookies meant giving up two Saturdays plus a little hustling on the side, for another twelve hours at least.

Every school has a fundraiser. We all know they are an important part of every school's budget. At our daughter's school, from the first day of class to the event in May there is a push to get everyone to commit to some committee. Chalk off another fifteen hours a year on that one.

Each class requires some parental involvement—back-to-school night, Christmas pageants, parent–teacher conferences. Some parents enjoy helping out in the classroom or the library. This time commitment can range from ten to fifty hours a year, depending on one's involvement. And some young kids have been known to beg their mothers to drive them to one of their class's field trips: six hours per trip, but at least there are some laughs with the other mothers.

Tee-ball or soccer general requires one practice per week and a game—roughly twenty-four hours a month. With age the practices go up to two per week. The bonus is the pizza party after a win. (I don't count that time—fun doesn't count.)

If your child takes art classes, ballet, karate, piano, skating, or gymnastics, add another eight hours per class per month. That's a lot of schlepping—not to mention money.

Got a kid with crooked teeth? That's only once a month and usually only for two hours, not counting driving time.

Most moms may find themselves going nuts occasionally trying to remember who's doing the pickup today at 3:00 P.M. (Or is it 2:30 this semester? Or is it 1:30 because today is Friday? Wait a minute—is there a Brownie meeting today?!) One mother I know has a calendar on her refrigerator with her daughter's schedule on it.

Many working mothers have to resign themselves to the fact that their children will be in on-site daycare at their school until Mom can get there. Bedlam breaks loose when the pickup parent has an emergency at work. Backup systems go into effect, favors are asked and later returned. Working mothers with latchkey kids undoubtedly pray every night.

When school children are sick not only do they need to be nursed back to health, but they still have to make up all the work that wasn't done when they missed school. When our daughter was recovering from pneumonia, we were glued together for ten days. While it was a serious illness, it required about the same amount of care that goes into most childhood maladies. And when kids are sick, they want Mommy. I was fortunate enough to have the time to spend with her, but what does the working mother do? Harriet told me:

> Hey, you go to work when you're sick as a dog. Then when your kid's sick, you use one of your sick days.

Unfortunately, this is the plight of the working mother. And the older mother often finds her physical resiliance is not what it used to be.

Summer proves to be the ultimate challenge. Summer camp is often the only solution. And sometimes kids don't want to go. They want those lazy, hazy, crazy days of summer. This is another problem for the working mom. Susan told me:

> I let my son go on a field trip to a major theme park even though in my heart I was worried sick about it. I didn't like the idea of him being stuck on a bus without a seat belt on a busy freeway for four hours round trip. And I didn't feel real comfortable that some teenage camp counselors would be capable of adequately keeping an eye on a bunch of young kids. But what I also had to contend with was a little boy who wasn't thrilled about going to camp every day, and this once-a-week field trip was at least something he looked forward to. It helped make camp palatable for him, so I let him do it.

These adjustment seem to be time-oriented. Most of the children of these women have yet to reach the minefields of puberty. However, some of my friends whose children now drive talk with nostalgia of this phase; children driving brings a whole new set of anxieties to parents. Mothers in chauffeuring stage talk about developing car-phobia. Candy, one mother, said:

> I spend more time shuttling kids around in the car than I ever thought humanly possible—from school to Brownies to tee-ball to dentists. It never ends. And weekends are just as bad. We go from games to birthday parties to the park. It just seems to escalate with each year. I can't wait till she can drive. I've only got seven years to go.

My mother always cautioned me about wishing my life away. The advantage to being the age I am is that I tell myself that this is only a phase in my life. It won't last forever. So despite the twelve thousand miles I'm putting on my car each year, I'm not complaining. These are relatively easy adjustments.

Some adjustments are more serious. Older parents must make many personal adjustments, especially concerning their mates. Said Katherine:

> My husband really wishes we could be traveling like some of our friends, but taking the kids to Venice, while it may be culturally stimulating and help them get a good grade in geography, is not how I want to spend my vacation. It's way too costly to take two kids to Europe, and frankly I dream about a romantic trip with my husband. But I don't see how that can happen. There just isn't

anyone we can leave two kids with for a ten-day period. *That* would be too costly. I think we've definitely sacrificed our intimacy in order to have a family.

Most of the couples with whom I talked don't feel comfortable leaving their children for any extended period of time. Even when children are left in good hands, parents feel the need to check on them to make sure they're okay. Some parents who have waited so long for children suffer tremendous guilt when stealing even a two-day vacation away from their children. That inability to spend time alone means the relationship between husband and wife is often compromised. We become Mommy and Daddy, and too often our practical side outweighs our romantic side. Just going to a movie requires finding a babysitter, praying the child doesn't get sick, then paying for the sitter and the movie. You start to ask yourself, *Is a movie really worth thirty-five dollars?* Slowly you stop spending that private time together. This is one of the adjustments many parents make, and older parents seem even less inclined to make the effort to be alone. They'd rather rent a movie. I know—I'm a renter. But we do try to go away for our anniversary every year. Each year, as our daughter grows a little older, it becomes easier to do. This is one benefit of a child growing older and more independent.

Some adjustments later are positive ones, like the fact that my daughter can dress and wash herself. She can make her bed. She can pick up her room—sort of. She can set the table, tie her shoes, and brush her hair. Best of all, all the hard work of babyhood has become easier. I don't know if there is anything more loving than a seven- or eight-year-old. They adore you. They want to make you happy. They're honest, they're loving, and they're joyful about life. If that doesn't make parenting worthwhile, nothing will.

Chapter 11

Motherhood Isn't Always What You Thought It Would Be

Take One:

A pretty nursery. Pastel colored stuffed toys smiling down from a shelf. Curtains gently billowing in the breeze. The mother is sitting in a rocker quietly singing a familiar lullaby to her sweet child who is just about to drift into dreamland. *Cut!*

Take Two:

A disheveled nursery. Toys strewn about, clothes in small heaps in corners. The smell of dirty diapers wafts thru the room. The mother is pacing the room. We hear the sound of a baby wailing. That's more like it. Shoot the second one. *That's* reality.

First-Time Mothers, Last-Chance Babies

Welcome to *Motherhood, Part 1*. In this movie our heroine, Mom, discovers that motherhood is not what she expected. The child of her dreams went to the couple down the street. She brought home Nocturnal Baby, the baby who doesn't sleep at night and screams by day. Watch as our leading lady braves her way through *colic, teething, temper tantrums* and much, *much* more! (This movie will be shown in it's entirety starting at 4 A.M. nightly. WARNING: Parental discretion is advised due to strong language and partial nudity.)

Hind sight is indeed 20/20. What most of us expected motherhood to be as opposed to what *is* is eye-opening. We all came to parenting with different notions as to what it would be like. We each had a little movie playing in our minds, one with all the central characters in our life (Husband, Wife, and Baby) and a happily-ever-after plot. First time mothers are allowed this indulgence.

How different, though, *was* reality from the fantasy we created? For those of us who waited until later in life to have babies, those fantasies had been rummaging around in our heads for quite some time. I asked other mothers if the experience of late motherhood was what they'd expected it to be. Here's what they said.

Lee Ann told me,

> The experience of motherhood was *not* what I thought it would be. First of all, when I was in college I said that I would *never* have kids. I thought, sure, I'm gonna get all excited about what Johnny's written on the wall? No way. Then I had them and you know what? I think that *is* pretty exciting. But I remember when my first child was three weeks old and it suddenly all hit me. "How am I supposed to remember all the things I'm supposed

to do? I have to give her this and give her that." I thought, "I'll never do all this." Giving her a bath was a major thing. I had tremendous fear. Hey, I was gonna have to do this every day, it wasn't like escrow that closes in sixty or ninety days—this was *every day!*

Another new mother added,

I had no pre-conceived notions about parenting. I thought mothering was about an absolute connection and it is. The whole experience of mothering has to do with a *relationship*. And it's constantly changing.

Overall, the comments varied. While some made comments like, "I thought I would be blissful. It was horrible," or "It's *hard*—harder than I expected," others like Erin enjoyed the other end of the spectrum: "This is better than I *ever* could have imagined."

Nancy told me, "It was better and worse than I expected. Better in bonding but worse in the drastic life change."

And Laura said, "I had fantasies of weekends with all of us in bed together and that's pretty much what happens now."

Each of us follows a different road in the journey of motherhood, encountering emotional as well as physical challenges. Patricia reported,

I didn't know it would press all these buttons and throw me up against all these issues with myself. I'm grateful I'm this age because in my twenties I would not have known how to sort them out or

articulate them or get help for them. I wouldn't
have been as in touch with myself. The issues of
parenting have lead me to discoveries about myself that I wouldn't have had reasons to explore.
But it's not always a fun way to learn.

For some it is a lonely experience. Said Sandy, "It
seemed like I never saw an adult. I felt very isolated, like I
was living in a vacuum—for a *long* time."

I remember that feeling. Tiny babies require a great
deal more energy than you might expect. Even *showering*
was a complicated event when my baby was little. Make-
up was left untouched for at least four months. My big for-
ay into the world was a walk with the stroller to the
grocery store. That was the extent of my social life for a
short time. But it didn't feel so short when it was happening. Since I'd never been through parenthood before I
didn't know if this was simply a stage or my new life. Having more than one child must be easier, because the second time you know that all you have to do is endure and
you'll eventually come out the other end.

Ann told me,

I didn't come into parenting with any preconceived notions. I hadn't baby-sat a day in my life.
In fact, the first infant I ever held was one week
before our daughter was born. I didn't have a clue
what to expect. I found the first six months to be
terrifying. She was a difficult infant and cried all
night. Luckily my husband was a wonderful
balance.

Frankie told a different story:

My pregnancy was a complete accident. It was very hard to grasp. I was forty-two when he was born and while I don't regret it, I wasn't prepared. I had *never* contemplated being a mother and I didn't chose to be a mother. I just got pregnant. We were thrilled with the idea of having a baby—it was the *reality* that set us back.

I, on the other hand, *did* want to be a mother and my pregnancy was as planned as the Normandy Invasion. But like Frankie, I too was set back by the reality. Which just goes to show, you never know until you get there. But in fairness, and all joking aside, while much of parenting didn't fit my mental fantasies, many of it's joys far exceeded it.

Some of the time my own journey was a rocky road—sometimes serious, sometimes humorous. I always dreamed of people cooing over my baby. When she was two months old (it was then Christmastime) a dear friend gave her a Santa suit in which she looked adorable. My mother and I took her to the mall to finish our Christmas shopping and she practically stopped traffic. *Everyone* it seemed was enchanted by this tiny baby dressed like Santa. When we were ready to leave, we walked out through a big department store at the end of the mall. That's when I overheard one woman say conspiratorally to another, "Oh, that's the baby I heard about!" Now, come on, even in my dreams I couldn't have thought that one up!

Part III

The Practical Side

Chapter 12

Sandwiched

"Parents lend children their experience and a vicarious memory; children endow their parents with a vicarious immortality."
—George Santayana

Advances in modern medicine have not only allowed us to have children later in life, but it has also benefitted that portion of the population who are older than us—our parents. The average life expectancy in the United States is now said to be around seventy-five years of age. And while the quality of life is what is important to all of us, sometimes what we are left with in our later life is a quantity of years, the quality of which is questionable—years in which beloved parents may need our care and attention.

When we talk about the strain having children later in life places on a family, we are usually thinking primarily of the energy required to run after a two-year-old. But what often gets overlooked is the energy not only to look after that two-year-old, but sometimes at the same time, to also care for an aging parent who may need as much attention as the child. Says Carol, who is caring for both an ailing mother and a toddler at the same time, "Sometimes I've seen my mother act worse than my child. It's very disconcerting."

Unlike most young couples whose parents are, for the most part, healthy and active, many of today's older couples who are contemplating parenthood must also consider their parents' present or future needs. Today, couples who become parents late face the distinct possibility of being part of the sandwich generation: raising one generation while caring for another.

According to the Los Angeles Times:

> The U.S. Census Bureau estimated in 1991 that 35% of the country's population had aging parents and children at the same time. The Washington Post reported in 1990 that nearly four million people had a frail elderly parent and a child under the age of fifteen. Many experts expect that number to increase as the whole population continues to age.

Certainly none of us has a crystal ball to predict what each individual's fate will be. Consequently older couples thinking about having children must move forward in faith, hoping they will be equipped to handle whatever is in store. There is no doubt that caring for your elderly parent while also raising a child is extremely stressful.

Joan Shapiro, Ph.D. in Clinical Psychology states,

> The negative side to older parenting is in regard to the generational sandwich. It is much harder when you are older to take care of the needs of elderly, frail parents and young active children. You

wind up exhausted.

Said Ann, one woman to whom I spoke,

Caring for my daughter and my mom at the same time, *and* working made me crazy. Mom was in and out of the hospital and sometimes we'd have to take her to the emergency room in the middle of the night and I'd have to bundle the baby up and take her with us. It was not the way I had wanted to start out my motherhood, but there it was. And I have to admit that while it was hard on me, I really believe Mom stuck around another year just to be with her newest grandchild. They were very close.

Ann also reported that getting up in the middle of the night for both her mother and daughter was physically exhausting as well as emotionally draining. Sometimes she didn't know who to go to first. Juggling all the various responsibilities is hard.

Said Susan, another late mother,

I knew always that my first responsibility was to the baby. She always came first. After that came my mom. I found that my husband came last. [My mother] was frail and I knew she needed me and he just got short shrift. Of course, I came in last, if I came in at all.

As a couple we often rely upon our mates to help us out. When both sets of parents are elderly it is twice the strain, because the person you've come to count on (your mate) is also drained. While every couple handles the responsibilities differently, many use the unspoken, "Your parents are your responsibility" method.

Said Toni,

> I was conscious of the fact that Mother was my responsibility, not my husband's. I only ever asked him to take her to a doctor's appointment after I had called on my brothers. I really felt she was our responsibility, not the responsibility of the in-laws. Now that his folks are both going into a senior apartment complex that has some medical supervision, I feel it's his job to oversee their care.

Even mixed generations who have gotten along well have conflicts. Parents have a way of "getting to us" that is unlike anything anyone else does. Can anyone doubt the reality of the strong unspoken dialogue that goes on within families, the messages that we each have responded to for decades that no one outside of the family hears? Those old buttons are still pressed regardless of our age or our parents' state of health.

Beth told me,

> My husband thinks my mother is funny and tells me I should be nicer to her, but he's not as plugged into her as I am. She keeps telling me in subtle ways that she wants more from me than I can give her. But I have a child and a husband I am responsible for also. I try to tell her that sometimes my son has to come first, and I know she isn't thrilled. But I'm doing the best I can.

When our parent are needy their state takes an emotional toll on us as well as them. But the physical toll is equally difficult. When a parent needs constant attention, sometimes it's hard to decide what's easier: having them live in your house or somewhere else. When my mother-in-law lived with us, her fears as well as her declining health kept her awake most of the night. She would call for either my husband or I ten to twenty times a night. She needed reassurance, but after some months of this we knew it was taking a major toll on our health as well.

We had a tough decision to make. For me, the decision was not complicated by years of emotional involvement. For my husband, it was. Ultimately, it was his decision to make. We were lucky in that we found a home for her that was nearby and allowed for frequent visits. For us, it was the right move. For Faith, another mom with whom I talked, having her mother live nearby was the best decision for her family, too.

> I stop by at least every other day, if not every day. Mother is living on her own, which isn't always good. Luckily, she now qualifies for having a nurse come by every day and that's been a big help. Before she had a nurse, among other things I was bathing my mother, which was a difficult maneuver. She also had some incidents where she lost control of her bowels; I was cleaning her diapers and my child's.

When an elderly parent needs hospitalization, often times the spouse is in equally bad shape as the one in the hospital. Georgia confessed,

> I went back home to care for my mother when she went into the hospital for back surgery. She had been having a rough time for quite a while, so

the house was not its usual tidy self—which I'd expected. What I *didn't* expect was the state my father was in. He'd lost ten pounds and looked totally lost. I spent the first day just ironing his shirts and cooking something for him to eat. I was trying to give him a sense that everything was back under control again. He needed to be cared for, too.

While the emotional and physical toll can be tremendous, the financial strain can cause hardship as well. In the United States, we do not have adequate government-subsidized help to assist in caring for our elderly. Medicare has limits as to what it will pay; the remainder becomes the family's responsibility. The supplemental costs have to be absorbed either by the savings of the elderly or that of their children.

For mature couples, these responsibilities are an important component in any decision-making process regarding having a baby later in life. But they should not deter anyone from the life-affirming act of having a child. While older grandparents may not be up to heavy-duty babysitting responsibilities, their love, like ours, is often richer for the wait.

Said Helen, one grandmother,

I never thought I would live to see my daughter's daughter. She was older, you see, when she finally got married. I'd pretty much given up hope. But I got lucky. And you know what they say about grandkids, that they are twice yours? It's true. You love them *doubly*.

And with that, she smiled and pulled out the photos to prove it.

Chapter 13

Financially Speaking

While years ago parents prided themselves on saving for their child's college education, nowadays late parents may have to pay the same amount as their college education cost to send their child to preschool and kindergarten. And the end is not in sight.

As educators interviewed for this book attested, older parents tend to be the strongest believers in the value of good education. Being in the work force for a considerable amount of time has given them the knowledge that education provides the edge in the job market. And parents interviewed for this book backed what the educators were saying.

Before I went off to college, there was much debate in my family over the wisdom of sending a girl to college. A few people felt a typing course would hold me in good stead when it came to looking for a job (this actually has been handy, but not in the way they anticipated!). Since I was only going to wind up with a job until I found a husband to care for me, why, for heaven's sake, blow all that money? Today that kind of conversation would be considered anachronistic. Luckily for me, my parents believed in education and didn't heed that consensus view.

In the future it appears as though our daughters will all be working. Both men and women are hopefully pushing the boundaries aside and allowing for individual expression for everyone, which means that the education of all our children to their fullest potential is a must. However, education costs money. And giving a child an education isn't the only financial strain late children place on a family.

Young couples rarely think about retirement. It is so far in the future that it seems foolish to dwell on. On the other hand, couples who may be in their forties or fifties when they have a baby may have already been giving it some serious consideration. Some have even roughed out where they may want to wind up. But retirement communities have yet to include toddler's pools in their brochures as a selling point. The future that some of us have dreamed about suddenly has changed. Rather than envisioning palm trees and golf courses we see jungle gyms and college campuses.

Nothing should ever hold anyone back from fulfilling a dream, but I know that when we decided to have Elizabeth (my dream) my husband essentially sacrificed what should have been his savings for his retirement years—as well as some of those years—to give me that dream.

It has affected every element of our lives. For example, when we go to visit my parents at their retirement community, we meet people who are my husband's age who are living the life he could be leading. He has had to postpone his retirement dreams for another ten years at least. And then we have to hope we can afford it. While he can't imagine his life without Elizabeth and says he wouldn't want to, sometimes he can't imagine being able to retire either!

My husband may have to wait a bit longer to retire, but I think the special love he receives from his youngest daughter more than compensates for the wait. He seems to get a special kick out of correcting someone who asks him about his beautiful granddaughter. "Oh no," he's happy to say, "she's my daughter!" And maybe it's only my imagination, but I think his chest swells just a wee bit.

Mercedes, the wealthiest woman I interviewed for this book, surprised me when I asked her what her biggest fears for the future were. "Money," she replied. "I worry that there won't be enough for his education. Don't you worry about not having enough?"

Actually, I don't, but I do recognize the validity of what she's saying and maybe my lack of concern is folly. We just heard about a couple who sold their house to finance their daughter's college education.

Education and retirement are only two financial concerns a late family has to consider. As medical costs increase and insurance coverage doesn't, families are well advised to look at a variety of health care packages that include the needs of an older family with young children. Yesterday our dentist told me Elizabeth needs to meet with the orthodontist. Today I'm finding out if it's covered by our insurance. If it isn't, it can be very costly.

Future costs also include all the various things we all know are bound to come up—stylish clothing, new bikes, piano lessons, school trips, camp, and proms. One mother I know has a budding skater on her hands and the cost of coaches, outfits, competitions (not to mention the wear and tear of getting to an ice rink every morning at six A.M. and sitting there for two hours) is phenomenal. Parents have always sacrificed greatly for their children, but they usually had a number of years to recoup once the children had left the nest. That luxury is gone for those who have children later in life. That, as they say, is an economic reality.

All parents regardless of age have a responsibility to their families in case they fall ill or die. However, for older parents, more so than younger parents, a will and financial contingency plan is a necessity. Older parents, aware that their ages may be a liability, do well to insure the financial safety of their families as well as providing a guardian for their children. When Bert died this year of a heart attack, it was a shock despite his age. His wife Barbara, a late mother, is now left with two small children. Hopefully they had a contingency plan to at least adequately take care of the financial needs of the family. On the plus side, older parents may be in a better financial position than their younger counterparts in planning how to care for children if a tragedy should strike. Years in the work force, perhaps even a pension plan, helps enhance the financial positions of some of those considering parenting.

Both a lawyer for estate planning and a qualified accountant, stock broker, or even your local banker can sit down with you and help make some long term plans that can help you achieve a future for yourself and your children that's as responsible and financially stress-free as possible.

Being older obligates us to be responsible for more than just our family's care and financial future. As older parents, our physical well-being is now our greatest asset. Thanks to our young children, we have even more of an obligation to ensure the state of our health. Those dreaded yearly check-ups with the doctor should no longer be considered optional; they are an investment in our future and the future of our children. And of all the investments we make, older parents should give their children the greatest gift of all, the one with the highest yield and the best dividends—ourselves.

Chapter 14

What the Educators Say

Seeing ourselves as others see us is good and instructive. Without the knowledge imparted by others we might not have a clear picture of how we are doing as parents. Certainly our individual experiences are often clouded by our fears, our love, and our prejudices. And while another person's opinion truly isn't of importance in the whole scheme of our parenting, their objectivity may prove very helpful. Hence the value of parent/teachers conferences; we are anxious to see how our child is doing in the world. Our child's teacher gives us the first glimpse into the person the rest of the world sees. A world that does not wear "parent-colored glasses."

Teachers still come in all sizes, shapes, and colors and today the same is true with parents. In earlier eras it was unusual to have parents over forty years of age delivering their child to the kindergarten for the first day of school. Now teachers shake the hands of some gray-haired or lined-faced parents. And while the teachers used to be the same age as or older than parents, now the parents are often older than the teachers! This is the result of the growing number of older parents. Deedee Hudnutt, an Admissions Director of a private K-6 school and who is herself in her forties, had this to say:

> I had a meeting last week with perspective kinder-garten families and basically I was looking at a group of my peers. I had my kids right out of col-lege and now they're teenagers. I was unusual among my friends back then. But what surprises me most now about these new families is that it's no longer the older husband–younger wife second marriage kind of thing that I'd expected. Many of the families I interviewed were of similar ages and had been married quite a while. Some parents re-ferred to these kids as their "miracle babies." And I find that the older fathers are often rearranging their work schedules so that they only have to work three or four days a week. They want to spend time with their kids.

Working at a private school might account for some of what Deedee saw. But other educators in the public sec-tor interviewed said roughly the same thing. It is appropri-ate here to point out that many late parents opt to send their children to private schools. Without question, the cost of private schooling is something that older parents usually have an easier time affording. Parents who are older are generally firmly established in the work place and therefore may have more income. Private schools can be very costly indeed. But when you've waited so long, and if you can afford it, many late parents feel there's nothing better that they can give their children than a good education. Private school is so obviously an economic privilege of the older parent that Deedee continued, "We are now targeting younger parents so as to balance the make-up of the class."

But what kind of an impact do we older parents have on the school systems that our children are invading and what impact, if any, will we have on the future of education? Are we more demanding, more difficult? The various educators of the schools I interviewed for this book all had encouraging and enlightening things to say about how we are faring. Says Bill Badham, a former principal of an elementary school,

> I've found that older parents, because of their maturity, know the value of an education and want their kids to have a good one. Generally, younger parents who haven't been in the work force that long may not believe it's necessary to have a college education. I find that older parents know just how important it really is.

There is a perception that older parents are more protective than younger parents. Some parents worry they may be asking too many questions of the school or the teacher. And because they've never been a parent before, there's no way of knowing what's considered "too protective." I asked Jim Lusby, an educator for the past twenty years and currently a grade-school principal, and here's what he had to say:

I think older parents are getting a bad rap. Frankly,
I don't see them as any more protective than younger parents. Parents, across the board, are more
protective today than they were twenty years ago.
The *era* we live in necessitates a more cautious attitude on the part of parents. Statistics of teenage
suicides, the number of weapons which find their
ways into schools, things like that tend to make
parents as a whole say, "gee, things have changed" and so they're *all* more protective.

There is also a notion that older parents want their
kids to do well in everything. We've all heard about the
kid who's after-school activities are daunting; computer
on Monday, piano on Tuesday, tennis on Wednesday, and
so on through the week. Is it true? Are we mature mothers
and fathers, driving our kids to excel? Here's the opinion
of Betsey Hale, a preschool director:

As far as I can see, these kids are *less* inclined to
ulcers than those of younger parents. These older
parents seem more relaxed. They want to stop and
smell the roses. Who wants to raise another lawyer? It's much more important to enjoy yourself
and be happy and these parents know it.

Some are concerned that being older makes parents
more inflexible, and that this inflexibility makes for stub-
born parents who make demands on the schools. Yet my
findings contradict this. Jim Lusby continued,

That's another myth. I find that older parents are
more open than younger ones to discussion about
their kids. Younger parents show a more

immediate gratification need than younger parents. They sometimes come in and want the school to change a certain program to meet their child's particular needs. For example: Tommy is not reading but the parents want him to. We believe that by the end of first grade Tommy will be reading and explained why. The younger parents will tend not to accept the explanation. The older parents, by virtue of experience, usually trust what you tell them. They understand the value of giving something time to work itself out. Older parents are more circumspect; experience has given them a perspective. They're no less demanding, but they're certainly more willing to get into a discussion.

It has been said that sometimes we late parents want to do everything for our youngsters. But does that mean that we will cripple them? Will they be ill-prepared for the real world? Again the results of my interviews contradict this. Bill Badham elaborated:

These older parents know what they need to *do* for a youngster. They know better what's involved. They've worked and probably had a few hard knocks and know how hard it is to make money and also know the value of an education. Young parents just don't have that experience yet.

Older parents are usually more settled in both their marital and work life. The stability of older parents is overlooked. How does that affect our parenting? Said Tom Hudnutt, director of a high school,

Children of older parents are probably going to be raised in a much more stable environment. The energy I spent in my twenties and thirties helped get me ahead but it meant moving my kids out of a school they liked. Ideally kids should stay in the same elementary school for the duration. Older parents probably can provide that stable environment. But then, maybe it would be boring. I don't know.

But on the subject of older parents being more demanding, an area where there seems to be much concern, John Eby, a primary school teacher, had this to say:

Older parents *aren't* more demanding primarily because they are less susceptible to performance anxiety. They don't feel the need to live through their children whereas younger people see their children as referenda on their adulthood and are less likely to have things in perspective.

When asked about the possibility of these children being more spoiled, Tom Hudnutt's reply was, "Older parents are probably more financially stable and, therefore, are more able to do what most other parents would *love* to do."

Educators today agree that the speed of change and the pace of life today are a challenge for *all* parents. But Mr. Hudnutt was concerned about how the older, more settled parents will handle their children when they reach the teenage years.

I wonder if a late-in-life parent wouldn't look at an adolescent as a creature from Mars. And what about a teenager who comes home drunk or wants to move out of the house? I wonder about the flexibility of that older parent.

But he does offer a counter-balance that is reassuring:

It's kind of a double-edged sword. While on the one hand you might have an older parent who is not as flexible, on the other you also have a parent who is probably more professionally, experientially, and spiritually rooted to address these issues.

And so what pitfalls do we older parents have to look out for? The educators I spoke with all expressed their concern for parents who are not exercising their parental roles. And that seemed to be an across-the-board kind of problem that affects parents of all ages. Bill Badham said, "In the 1960s Benjamin Spock began this new age of permissiveness. It's gone too far, that's for sure." And Jim Lusby elaborated,

The societal norm, which has developed over the past twenty-five years, is that we want *everyone* to evolve in their own way. We want *everyone* to be free. We don't want to impinge on *anyone's* rights. What we forget is that our children's rights are impinged on every day by MTV and movies and what their peers tell them. But parents are afraid to tell their kids to eat their peas. It's an abdication of their parental responsibilities. They're not clear about what they should be in the lives of their children.

Parenting has certainly changed from the way we

were raised, but then our entire society has undergone a major transition. Mothers, fathers, men, women, and parenting are no longer the clear-cut roles they once were. By and large, parents today are sometimes confused about what to do. Tom Hudnutt offers this guidance:

> The problem is that parents think they are raising children and they're not. They're raising adults. That's their mission. We have to think more about what our kids are going to be like at thirty years old than at eight years old.

When questioned how one defines that difference, he continued,

> You expect adults to operate with a certain amount of autonomy and you don't expect to live your life thru an adult. I think we are much less performance anxiety-ridden about other adults than we are about our children. We are very forgiving of the shortcomings of other people's children but not so of our own. We are more forgiving of differences in physical growth rates than intellectual ones. If the kid next door learns to ride a bike before our child, it's okay, but if the neighbor can read at four we feel threatened.

The results of my research seem to show that we older parents are able, by virtue of our maturity, to allow our children to be who *they* are—not an extension of ourselves. I was fully prepared to meet these educators and hear how over-protective and over-indulgent we are as older parents. What I came away with was a strong report that we're doing an excellent job.

Chapter 15

What the Shrinks Say

What makes a good parent? How can we assert which people may indeed be better equipped? Is it not presumptive to claim a superior ability in something so personal as parenting, something that is wholly dependent upon *who* does the job of parenting? And who can judge what is good parenting versus better parenting?

During the past twenty years, the field of childhood development and psychology has greatly expanded. Television, newspapers, and magazines are filled with an abundance of studies. Books attesting to different child-rearing philosophies jam the book shelves so that only the most stubbornly unaware could remain ignorant to all this readily available information. And like Pandora's Box, a myriad of child-rearing philosophies, theories and ideologies have spilled out. Some people feel these new studies have accounted for the enormous adjustments we've made in the way we treat our children. While parents in the past could honestly plead ignorance to the effects certain types of behavior had upon their children, our generation has been alerted almost to the point of inertia. Often we don't know which route to follow or to whom we should listen. How does a layman separate data from theory?

Since doing a good job is a top priority for older parents, I asked a variety of experts to help define good parenting. I spoke with Marriage, Family, and Child Counselors, Ph.D.'s in Child Psychology, school counselors, and psychologists.

Lee Kroeger, M.F.C.C. said, "A good parent is someone capable of letting the kid *be* and setting the right boundaries, which would seem paradoxically opposed or impossible to figure out how to do." Letting a child be his or her own unique self seems to be a fairly easy assignment. Nowadays the prevailing tone of parenting leans towards that. Setting the right boundaries, however, is a whole other matter. How do I know what those correct boundaries are? Who has the answers? Lee Kroeger's response is simply, "That's the tough part."

I asked Dr. Judith Warren, a clinical psychologist, what her definition of a good parent was.

Someone who is able to love the child as a separate being and not as an extension of his or her self.

Would being older help in that? Here's what she replied.

For the most part being older *would* help because you've had time to work things out and you generally have a better sense of yourself. Most of the women in my practice are in their twenties and thirties and it seems that the more educated women are waiting nowadays to have children.

Cornelia Hansen, M.F.C.C., who specializes in family therapy, defined a good parent this way:

Someone who recognizes the fact that the child is an individual who has been placed in the parents custody. And like a good gardener, you must provide nurturing and stimulation while allowing a child to express his or her own uniqueness, and being excepting of that uniqueness. But the parent also has to provide a structure with flexible limits.

Joan Shapiro, Ph.D. in Clinical Psychology and a high school guidance counselor, had another definition of a good parent:

One who is emotionally stable enough to provide nurturance and encourage a child's self-esteem—and supports it. One who sets appropriate limits and who's free enough to express his or her love.

Nearly all the professionals interviewed warned that what they see over and over are parents who are not setting limits. When I asked Dr. Shapiro about those limits she said, "A parent needs to set boundaries as to what's okay and not okay to do and to set those limits in a firm but respectful way."

I questioned her about boundaries. Aren't my boundaries different from someone else's, and where *did* I develop my boundaries? "We usually parent as a reaction or
a re-creation to how we were parented," she explained.

Why does our generation seem to have difficulty setting boundaries? According to Dr. Shapiro,

> I have talked to so many parents who have trouble
> setting boundaries, and what it comes down to is
> that to set boundaries you have to be clear about
> what your values are. I can not tell a parent what
> their values are; they have to decide that for them-
> selves. And many people simply do not have clear-
> cut values.

I asked her if older parents had any advantage in this
regard.

> The older you are the more of a perspective you
> have. You have more life experiences and you
> have probably settled down. Your work situation is
> most likely defined. You also have a longer history
> in the marriage of being able to work issues out.
> There is a certain amount of wisdom that comes
> with age. Having children forces you to articulate
> your values, and the older you are the more of a
> perspective you have. A lot of older parents who
> come up to me after lectures seem to carry a cer-
> tain guilt with their parenting. They want to do the
> job so perfectly, and I assure them everyone
> makes mistakes. I also tell them that unless you do
> major things wrong consistently, your kids will
> bounce back; you'll raise a good kid.

Cornelia Hansen, M.F.C.C., had this to say about parenting styles:

Most people choose their parenting styles usually as some sort of reaction to the way they were raised.

Psychologists are careful to point out that the success of parenting is wholly dependent on the individual *doing* the parenting. Says Ron McDevitt, Ph.D.:

The quality of mothering is affected by many other things than age—the kind of family you were from, what your general level of emotional well-being is, how supportive your husband is—these are some of the things that will affect how good a parent you will be. And undoubtedly, how motivated you are will affect how good a parent you will be also.

Dr. McDevitt elaborated on some of the components of successful parenting.

There are many variables in successful parenting. Age is not an insignificant one. But there are other elements that also factor in—cultural rearing, education, economics—these are all powerful influences.

Successful parenting also has to do with "fit." So says Lynn Kessler, Ph.D.,

It's been my experience that what's most important is the goodness of fit between the temperament of the parent and the temperament of the child. Researchers did a study and they placed kids into three different categories: easy, difficult, and slow to warm up. That was the temperament that pretty much followed them through their lives. My experience has been that if you have a very out-going, gregarious, extroverted type mother and you have a very laid-back, easy-going kid, it sometimes is not a good fit. It can create a lot of problems for the parents (and child) unless the parent is very willing to say, "This kid is nothing like me. Let's see what I can do to adjust my needs and wants to meet the kid that I actually have." And I think that an older parent may be more aware and more willing to make those adjustments.

What seems clear is that the age at which one begins parenting is not the only thing to consider when deciding whether or not to have a child. Says Dr. McDevitt, "A sensible evaluation of the options should be what helps decide whether or not one is too old to parent."

Maturity helps one make a clear evaluation of all those options. Understanding our own needs and setting them next to the needs of a child takes a certain level of maturity and a willingness to make important judgment calls. At a junior high graduation party several years ago, the parents who owned the home in which the party was held offered beer to the fourteen- and fifteen-year-old youngsters. While the younger parents went along with this, one of the older parents stood up and protested. Still, even older parents sometimes have problems assessing situations, as Donna makes clear.

My biggest challenge lately seems to be figuring out when it's time to *do* something about a problem. When is it a real problem, and when is it just . . . life? When should we be sympathetic and indulgent, when should we make a kid tough things out? When is their unhappiness something serious, when is it just the good old blues?

These are the tough calls. No child comes with a maintenance book to let you know exactly what this particular individual will need to turn into a happy, successful adult. Much of the emotional damage adults live with is the result of their parents, whose choices did not suit their particular needs. And while it may sound wonderful when a parent exclaims that they treat all their children the same, the reality is that no two human beings *are* the same, and probably nothing could be worse than to treat two individuals exactly alike. So, like Donna, the hard part is figuring out when to do what—and praying you make the right choice.

But societal prejudice and private fears are two different things. While we can see ourselves coming and going, as older parents we may still fret privately about being "too old." Says Lynn Kessler, Ph.D., a Marriage, Family and Child Counselor,

> Don't misread it when your child says to you "Oh, Mommy, you have wrinkles." You're old to a child when you're twenty-five. Parents have to be careful not to internalize what their kids say to them.

Successfully parenting a child takes a certain level of maturity, and conscientious parenting means being aware of the commitments to that child. Age is merely one factor of our parenting. What is far more important seems to be the prevailing wisdom on parenting. Dr. Kessler sums up the opinion of many when she comments, "What is important is nurturing the individual that is your child."

Chapter 16

What the Siblings Say

Blended families are not as perfectly matched as they appear on television. Generally, a great deal of emotional pain is endured in the process of making the transition into the "new" family. Old resentments, unfulfilled expectations, and unresolved conflicts all add to the fertile backdrop of the new family. These children have had quite a full plate already; the divorce of their parents, the adjustment to shuttling between both parents, the one parent finding a new love, the marriage, and finally, the new "parent" in the home. Adding a sibling, who could possibly take even more energy away from Mom or Dad, is a potentially volatile issue. While remarriage might put an end to a child's dream of the biological family reuniting, the birth of a baby to the new couple obliterates it completely. It would be no small wonder then to find a great deal of resentment on the part of the original children.

Two of my closest and dearest friends are my stepdaughters, Julie and Catherine. They are more precious to me than they will ever know. They gave me my first dry run at parenting, which I was allowed to do without the full responsibility that their own father and mother shouldered. They taught me how vulnerable a child can be and how important it is to be heard and loved.

Our relationship has not always been this glorious. We have all worked very hard over the years to develop the rapport we now enjoy. But luckily for us, the blend *did* happen. And the birth of Elizabeth helped form us into a united family.

For years now, we have all grumbled to one another about how much we hate the word "step" which gets attached to our relationship. The dictionary defines steps as "a short distance." I am their *step*mom, they are my *step*children. While I have never wanted to usurp the excellent position their mother holds in their lives, I *hate* being a step*anything*. There's a negative connotation in being a stepmother or stepchild. You're a little (or a lot) removed from the object of desire. If I simply refer to them by their first names it fails to let a stranger know that these people are a part of my immediate family. If I attach the dreaded "stepchild" moniker I am always fearful that I am giving out a subtle message that might be interpreted as "Hey, I'm not responsible for these guys!" and, therefore, distance myself from them. Nothing could be more inaccurate in my household.

What helped to bond us as a family was the introduction of this tiny baby who was part of each of us and who suddenly became the missing piece that gave us all an absolute, undeniable familial link. We had truly become a family. Catherine even said to me, "I even feel more connected to your folks (Elizabeth's grandparents) because of Elizabeth." Now we all have someone in common—someone who is precious to all of us.

One of the great pleasures in interviewing siblings was to hear the various feelings they had to share. I was surprised to find that the majority of those I talked with said the experience was happy and unifying. Where I expected to find deep resentment and anger, I found generosity and joy. Babies, it seems, do bring happiness.

Preparing a family for the introduction of a new child is important, however. While those interviewed seemed happy with the experience, experts advise that a conscious effort needs to be made by the parents to make sure old unresolved issues aren't being ignored.

Dr. Judith Warren, a clinical psychologist, says, "It's a myth to think that a new baby brings the family together. The new baby often can cause a lot of jealousy to surface." When asked what she thought would help the situation, she replied, "Lots and lots of talking. Feelings have to be discussed and brought out in the open."

Cornelia Hansen, MFCC, was asked how families should introduce a new step-sibling.

There are too many individual cases and no rules about how to do it right. A lot is dependent on the luck of who's involved. It's important for the family to be able to recognize if there's a problem and instead of being in denial, dealing with it. There has to be a willingness to share in the problem and a willingness to say, "I don't know everything."

Having a baby is the intimate decision made by two adults. But when those adults have other children—generally from a previous marriage—it is imperative to take the original children's feelings into account.

Geri and Tim explained,

> We talked a lot about the kids before we went ahead. They were a *major* concern. We weren't sure how they'd handle it. In the end we felt that if it felt right for us then it would probably be right for them. And luckily that's how it turned out. It's been great.

Perhaps it is in part due to their maturity, but the children of older parents may fare better than those of younger couples who remarry and bring in a child. The children are often older and more mature. Sometimes the therapy that was sought during transitional times has taught skills that produce better communication and, therefore, bad feelings don't get buried. But perhaps the most logical reason of all is simply the indomitable spirit of youth that wants, above all else, a happy ending. A wedding is a happy celebration of the union of two people. But their children are merely an auxiliary to that event. With the birth of a child, all members of the family share equal footing in the event. Some roles may be of greater importance, but *everyone* has a place. And therefore, everyone is needed.

However, if the child is part of a family that merely decided to try again later in life and add another member to the family, there is a whole other element involved. The picture of the old family, so firmly in place, is hard to recreate.

A mother who had a third child ten years after the

second recalled, "It had always been just the four of us and it seemed set in stone that that's what we were. We were a family of four. When I realized I wanted another I couldn't believe it." Her children couldn't believe it either.

None of the children interviewed felt that they were in any way a part of the decision to bring a new baby into the family. Tara admitted, "It never occurred to me that it was any of my business." And Michael put it this way: "I felt it was my business but not my choice."

Clara agreed. "I didn't feel included or excluded in the decision," she said, "Which is, I suppose, the way it is. The parents make the decision and the children are left to react."

Ava said,

Initially I was surprised by the idea of a baby in our family. We (the kids) were all so grown up. We'd never thought of babies, but my stepmom didn't have any and she wanted this one.

Chris added,

They didn't tell my stepbrother and I until my mom was three months pregnant, so it was really a surprise. But I was excited about it.

Nina said,

When Mom told us, my brother and I were both really surprised. Then we had a big fight over who was going to use the phone first to call our friends.

Though most of the overall feelings were happy, the children with whom I talked voiced some lingering fears.

I did worry what it would do to my relationship with my stepdad. I was his only girl up until that point. What if the baby was a girl and took my place?

Joan said,

It was a little hard because even though I was twelve at the time, I still thought of my mommy as *my* mommy and it was hard having to share her.

I asked the siblings I talked to if they were at all embarrassed by their older parent having a baby. These were some of the responses:

Embarrassed? No. I think it's a really '90s thing.

Not at all. I think it's great. When I tell them I have a little sister, most people think it's interesting and want to hear all about it. .

What's to be embarrassed about?

Not at all. Some people think it's strange, but I know a lot of my friends think it's neat.

When asked to describe the relationship with their sibling, the response was overwhelmingly positive.

Our relationship is very good. I know she adores me, it's really obvious. And I adore her. I feel really protective of her—I want everything to be smooth for her.

I think our relationship is very good. I don't know if it's the nine-year age difference—you know, being in totally different worlds—but I know she looks up to me.

Our relationship is really great. Now that I'm away at college, I really look forward to coming home and seeing him.

I was curious to know how the "new" family was raising the baby compared to how those interviewed perceived they had been raised. Here are some of the responses.

No comparison. She has better parents than I did—she *has* parents. I had absentee parents. Her parents are patient and encouraging and *there*.

My little sister is spoiled. She gets what she wants when she wants it. They're better in that they're a little looser. My mom had some strict rules with me when I was growing up, but my little sister doesn't have the same rules.

She gets a lot of what she wants. I have to work for something.

It's very different. For one thing there's more money in this family. There's more total attention to the child. Ours was a more traditional upbringing. I had brothers and sisters and Dad used to be at work quite a bit. That was back in the 1970s when you just *did* parenting. Now you have to do it *right*. You know, the nursery has to be black and white with a touch of red.

My Mom got a divorce when I was two and so I never lived in a traditional sort of family. I think it would be neat to have a family like in the movies, and I think my little brother has that.

The differences undoubtedly lead some siblings to observe the mistakes their parents make. For example:

Sometimes I think her not having to work for something she wants is a mistake.

They are not consistent with her. And I think giving her everything leads to a lack of appreciation for what she's got.

I wish in a way that she had brothers and sisters her own age. I think that's kind of unfortunate. It's fun to be born and have built-in friends. That's something we had that she doesn't. She has us but I mean someone her own age. But then she has some things that we *didn't* have.

I wish she had more physical outlets and that Dad didn't constantly remind her to not jump on the bed, you might get hurt—that kind of a thing. I don't want her to think the world is a dangerous place. That's so typical of Dad. But other than that, she's *totally* encouraged and anything she shows an interest in is explored.

He's a little spoiled, but then I think we all are.

Chapter 16

I asked if it was painful to witness their sibling getting what they may not have. Here's what some said.

Yeah. Not now but in the past and not even specifically. It's just seeing what good parenting is and I didn't have that. I think how different my life would have been if I'd had good parents from the start.

No! I think having another little girl for my mother to hold on to has made my life *easier*. I'm going to be able to leave and have my life. I think when I go off to college, though, it will be harder on my sister. The only thing I resent is that she gets too much.

When I was little, I adored my dad but he was never around, he was always working. And I missed him. Now he's around all the time with my sister. I guess that does make me a little sad for what might have been.

I have no resentment. None. I think she deserves all the best. I think it's great that my Dad is *here* for her. I never felt that my father doesn't love me but he loves her. I *know* he loves me.

It's very complicated because my parents went through a lot of crap to become who they are now. Had they just aged without all the incidents they went through, I don't know that they would have been different, but they went through a lot of painful growing and that's why they're cool now. There are always those moments though when there is

First-Time Mothers, Last-Chance Babies

resentment, especially when [my half-sister] was little, because she had great parents. But I think everything's pretty equitable now. I know that we're all supported and encouraged.

Having a baby in the family is a new experience for everyone. At the very least there was a nine-year age gap between those interviewed and their younger siblings. For some there was a twenty-one year gap. What did they learn about babies?

It's a lot more complicated than I thought.

It shouldn't be entered into lightly. It's just the most frightening thing. I had *no* idea what babies were like. And ours had colic! You practically have to be a saint. Luckily I could leave after babysitting.

I learned a lot of skills, that's for sure.

I learned how easily babies and children are influenced by those around them.

It made me realize what exactly is involved. I don't have a romantic view of having a child and that it's all beautiful—it's a *major* undertaking. I'm glad I had the experience, because I think I would have been in for a real shock. I was always glad when visiting that I could leave at the end of the day.

She was my first baby experience. It brought up a lot of feelings in me. I remember hearing her scream when she was a baby and feeling this rage and I thought, "If I ever do this, I'm gonna have to work this out."

Before I used to think that I wouldn't have children, but now I think I will—when the time is right.

After witnessing older parenting, I wondered if these siblings would recommend it.

Yeah, I think when you're older you're more ready to experience a child's life and willing to give over some of yours.

I can only go on the experience I've seen and to me it's an amazing example of good parenting. I have to assume that older parenting is a good thing.

When you're older and more financially secure I think you find it easier to take on the responsibility.

Recommend it? Yes, but by thirty-five and not forty, because of the energy required as well as the fact that I'd like to have two. I think it must be strange to not have [younger siblings] but that's because I did. A sibling is like being born with a friend.

Physically, it's better to have them when you're younger, but emotionally and financially it's better to have them older.

When you're younger and you're infatuated, you have a romantic notion about babies: "Oh, I want

to have your baby," and accidents [pregnancies]
happen. I don't think older people make that error
in judgment. I think it all goes back to the patience
thing. Young people are impatient. I know I'm not
patient enough now. For me, older will be better.

The dynamics that go into each blended family structure determine whether or not adding a new baby is a
happy experience. Hopefully the parents sensitivity to
their older children will help the transition. Said Dr. Joan
Shapiro, a clinical psychologist,

If parents spend the time and do the groundwork
so that the family is stable *prior* to introducing a
baby into the family, then you can have a very
happy occasion. But it requires lots of talk and the
airing of a lot of feelings.

Dr. Judith Warren, a clinical psychologist, talks about
much the same thing.

There can be a lot of jealousy when a new child is
born. Every new step (remarriage, birth) ends the
dream for the existing child of that child's biological parents getting back together. You just have to
do lots of talking, especially about when the older
child was born and what they were like. You have
to validate them and let them have their feelings.

For our family, the birth of Elizabeth marked the opening of a new chapter in all our lives. It helped delineate
the past from the present. And given that opportunity, we
were all allowed the chance to begin anew. And more
importantly, we were given the occasion to practice what

we'd all been learning—love. My young daughter may not have a little brother or sister to play with, but she has a level of love from her older sisters that will take her many years to appreciate.

The other night Elizabeth asked me, "Mom, are Julie and Catherine my half-sisters?" "Yes," I replied, "You have a different mommy than Julie and Catherine." "Mom," she retorted, "We're not *half!* We're *sisters!*" And I know what she means. I'm a step and she's a half. Which just goes to show, she doesn't like labels either!

Chapter 17

What the Fathers Say

Although many single older mothers are successfully parenting, no discussion of older parenting can take place without the inclusion and acknowledgement of the role the older father, when present, plays in the family portrait. The love, support, and joy a father brings to a home is an equally important influence on the children. No one can argue against the fact that the optimum environment in which to raise a child includes both mother and father. The Chinese call it yin and yang. In nature it is called balance. In our house, he's called "Budgie."

I adore my father, and so I came to parenting with a preconceived notion about how special a father can make a child feel. Once, when I was down with the measles, my father came home from work with a bunch of peonies. Just for me. When I was in the school play in high school, my father gave me a box of long stem red roses. I still keep the card that came with them. To this day, as I steadily approach fifty years of age, I am still "fathered"—and it is still special to me.

Lucky children tuck memories away of things that their parents did that made them feel special and loved. For most of those denied the affections of a father, the effects are profound and painful.

The difference between a mother's and a father's love is, of course, vast and wholly dependent on the individuals who generate that love. And while I always valued the gift of having two parents, I never understood the importance of the love given by both mother and father to a child. Then I had Elizabeth.

To our daughter, we are very clearly two halves of a whole. She never chooses one over the other. She may desire one of us more than the other at a particular moment, but that is usually due to a prior absence of one of us for whatever reason. Her security is dependent on having *both* of us in her world. This is certainly not to say that a great many children don't flourish under the guidance of a single parent; they obviously do. And it is a double role that those devoted parents undertake.

Over the past twenty-five years the role of father has gone through as dramatic a re-definition as that of mother. Previously fathers functioned as providers and authority figures. They were the head of the household, their responsibilities clearly defined. But with the shifting of women's roles, men too got a chance to look at what their fathering role had been and re-establish for themselves what kind of fathers they wished to be. And this new definition seems to be benefiting everyone. Mothers are now getting more help with the parenting responsibilities (though still, most women report that parenting duties are not *equally* shared). But without question, the involvement of fathers today is light years ahead of what our mothers generation experienced. Emotionally connected fathers benefit both father *and* child.

Fathers interviewed for this book provided a refreshingly upbeat look at the experience of older parenting. For each of them there was no question that they loved the experience. However, it was not an experience that was without some drawbacks, particularly when it came to the change parenting made in their relationship with their wives.

When asked about why they had children later in life, their responses were varied. Jake explained,

> We'd both been married before and we each had older children. I had a boy and she had a girl so it kind of looked perfect. I assumed she didn't want any more kids and she assumed I didn't. Besides, I didn't want to burden this "middle-aged" woman with *my* desire for another child. One day we finally admitted to each other that we did want a baby—*our* baby. We were both blown away with that discovery. It was amazing. It was so different this time around because *neither* of our older children had been a conscious choice. This baby was a *very* conscious choice.

Harvey's reason was different:

> Are you kidding? I couldn't commit to *lunch* when I was younger.

Even though the divorce rate is high in this country, many men are coming to their new marriages *without* having had children before. For those men these new marriages seem to open the door to a possibility never before desired. Bob said,

> I'd been married once before and I was very afraid of becoming a parent. I didn't want to have kids. I'd had an unhappy childhood and I was afraid I'd be the same kind of parent that I had. And I think if I had [parented] at twenty-five, I would have.

The years which elapsed between his first and second marriage, Bob reported, gave him the time to mature and face his fears about parenting.

Many divorced men, however, have children from a previous marriage and are not anxious to start all over again. A lot of them said they didn't want the possibility of being separated from yet another child, which had been so painful in their divorce. Still others felt they were done with parenting, or at least close to being done. Joel told me,

> I already had three teenagers from a previous marriage. I loved them very much and really looked forward to the time we spent together when they would come for the weekend. But I also *loved* the peace and quiet of our house when it was just the two of us and you could play classical music instead of listening to hard rock. I had no desire and no need for another child; mine were almost grown. But my wife had never been married before and she very much wanted a baby. The trouble was, I knew what we were getting into and

she didn't.

Occasionally, the reason for not having had a child was simple. Finding the right partner, particularly if you've spent time developing a career, sometimes proves difficult. Henry said, "I had my kids later simply because I hadn't found anyone I wanted to have children *with*."

Peter contributed, "I'm a late bloomer. It took a while until I finally met the right person."

Being older seemed to enhance the fathering skills of these men. Allan said,

> If I had had a child in my mid-twenties, I would not have gotten through all the identity problems and the career problems that are inherent to your twenties. When I was in my twenties I didn't know beans about life. I had a different perspective about life and what was important. I had to go through several relationships, among other things, to figure things out. It's not that in my late thirties it all miraculously paid off, but by the time I had my children I had certain things handled and that was *definitely* better for my kids.

David reported,

> Being younger was what cost me my first family. I didn't have my priorities straight. I was too worried about making a living and building up my career. By the time [my second wife and I] had my daughter I had totally changed my set of values.

Steve told me,

When I was younger I had to see the latest movie
and go to the newest restaurant. I know it sounds
corny and predictable, but when you get older
your priorities change. I'm no longer thinking
about *me*, I'm thinking of my family. It's very nice
to be *connected,* to have people who care about
me and who are in some way dependent on me.
Maybe it's the primordial need to be a part of a
group. I don't know.

Jerry put it this way: "I had to get rid of all my selfish
bones. You can't be selfish and have a family."
Tim had other reasons:

What hasn't killed us by this point has made us
wiser. I'm definitely wiser—and mellower. There's
no way you can't be more mature at forty than you
were at twenty. I think at this stage of life, you're in
the parenting mode, so to speak, you're willing
and capable of giving. You're so much more
equipped. Let me tell you something. I just had a
job offer that for *me* is better than the job I'm at
now. But it wasn't better for my family. There
wasn't the security, the benefits . . . so I turned it
down. It wasn't hard to do because my family is
what makes me feel whole and nourished, and
that's what counts.

Joel, who had gone through a divorce, commented,

The most difficult part of my divorce was breaking
the daily contact with my son. I worried that when
he found out [my second wife and I] were going
to have a baby that he would feel I was less

available to him. But this is his only sibling and luckily, right from the very beginning, he's been crazy about her and she about him. Having her bonded our family and allowed me the pleasure of watching my child grow up on a day-to-day basis, which I missed out on with him.

Bart, echoing the sentiments of a few second family fathers, said, "I got to do it right this time."

But for those who never had children before, the experience was a venture into the unknown. And for some, it tapped into the unexpressed.

Evan put late parenting in a new light when he mentioned the *male* biological clock:

When I heard that my wife was pregnant . . . somewhere in all the other emotions that were going on, I heard a big sigh of relief. Like, "Oh good, I get to be a dad." It was only then that I realized that something had been going on there—that there's a male biological clock ticking as well. It may not be as strong as a woman's, but it's there. Suddenly I realized that there were needs here that weren't being met. That there was this desire to do something and that I was probably going to cop out on it if left to my own devices. Footprints in the sand, leaving a legacy . . . You know those corny expressions but there's some truth to them—something that has to do with a very deep level of love. There's *never* been anything in my life that overwhelms me like the love I have for my children. God forbid I had missed it. What if I *hadn't* gone to the fair? Had I not bought a ticket and gotten on the ride, I would have been less a person for it. And that's what parenting does—it makes you greater than yourself.

Frank added,

We got married specifically to have a family. I wanted that sense of being part of a family—it's almost primal for me. I always knew I'd be a great dad, and I am. Hey, how many guys do you know who'd take three kids to the movies at 11 A.M. on a Saturday?

Delighting in the experience of parenting did not mean these men were unaware that some parts of older parenting were less than desirable. When questioned about the disadvantages to being older fathers their views were varied. Tom said,

Well, sometimes I think I'm the oldest father in her class. I can't do quite as many physical things as I used to when I was younger. (However, Tom's wife reported that he can still beat his sixteen-year-old at basketball!)

Ted observed,

My son has gotten me back in touch with the child in me. He's taught me that you can live life at a slower pace. We don't just go to the store for milk, we go on an adventure. We check out the worm, he asks me about the clouds, he wants to know why the man has a beard—a hundred questions. It's amazing.

Said Alex, "There are definitely more responsibilities on me, but would I change it? No."

Todd reflected,

It does affect your career, but actually that doesn't matter to me anymore. When I was younger my priorities were me and my career. When the kids were born it became home, wife, and children.

Marc elaborated on the same theme:

When I was younger I was very career-oriented. I had definite goals and things that I wanted to accomplish. But now I'm more concerned about enjoying myself. I don't want to work all kinds of crazy hours now. I want to go home. I want to see my children. I don't want to miss one little thing.

Clearly, these men seemed happier concentrating on the good side of parenting. When asked if there were any advantages to having children later there were many things that fathers cited.

Gary told me,

I can't think of one bad thing about having this child. I can't *imagine* life without her. She's great to come home to and she's wonderful to play with. Sitting and doing homework with her is fun because I get to watch her mind work.

Said Cal,

When I think how close I came to *not* having this child it frightens me. She's the best thing that ever happened to me.

Kyle commented,

> Because I'd been through it before, financially
> speaking, I didn't think, "Oh my god, what do we
> do?" I knew what we'd do and it was no big deal.
> Besides, I'm financially in a better position now
> than I was when I had my other child.

Though all the fathers acknowledged that they certainly felt the increased financial responsibility, they all felt that being older usually meant you had some kind of career stability. Ironically enough, three of the fathers interviewed were undergoing some level of career reevaluation. Two openly stated that much of what they were going through was directly the result of their new priorities.

The change from husband and wife to father and mother is one that concerns every couple contemplating parenting. The introduction of a baby to the twosome is fraught with fears of the unknown. The mature fathers interviewed were asked how having a baby had affected their marriage. Ivan said,

> I remember somebody once saying, "Relation-
> ships are like sharks—either they move or they
> die." I think that's it. The kids have kept our rela-
> tionship moving. I think all relationships need
> things to hold on to, and homes and children give
> you the handle to hold on to in the rough times.

Larry added,

I think it's been 50/50 good and bad. The good is the shared joy of experience. You know how they say seeing a sunset with someone else doubles your pleasure? Well, it's tripled when you add a child. But I am also aware that I gave up a deeper, more selfish relationship with my wife and I miss that.

Michael pointed out,

It's turned us into a family, and what could be better than that? I think our love and our commitment has significantly improved *because* we are sharing the experience of being parents.

Victor commented,

I'm looking forward to the day when the kids are grown and we can be alone. I think one of the pleasures of our later years will be the shared experience of raising our kids and hopefully seeing our grandchildren.

Jared said,

Having children has made our commitment so much deeper and it reinforces why you married this person, who's values you espouse and that you want imparted to your children. I love coming home to my family . . . not just my kids but the *family*. I think all the time that I'm a rich man. I just don't have any money.

Role models are as hard to find for men as for women

these days. Being a good father at a later age is difficult when no one has taught you how. Most of the fathers interviewed remembered their fathers as authoritarian and remote. Said Bill,

> With my parents it was, "We fed you, we clothed you, we educated you, see you around." Parenting to them was a duty. Children were a burden, I think. You know—the old "seen and not heard" routine. It was a big surprise to find out what a joy parenting is.

Jake put it this way,

> He was not the kind of guy who would hug you. I can't imagine not hugging my son. With my dad, if you wanted to talk, you were interrupting what he wanted to do—reading or watching TV—not being with us.

When discussing the emotional aspects of fathering, every father was eloquent in his discourse. Here's what some of them said.

Colan told me,

> One of the most exciting times in my life was the day I saw my daughter's first sonogram. I stood there and thought, *Here is this little person that was always meant to be*, and I thought, *Hey I haven't seen you in a long time. We're gonna be together soon*. And the first time I held her in the delivery room I felt that this little person was a part of me; finally, I was complete.

Phil explained,

I have this feeling that moments before my death one of my remembrances will be of my children's births. I was there. I was the first person to hold them, the first person to bathe them. I took their footprints. I welcomed them into this world. It was a way of letting a male into the mystery of the whole birth process. Birth is the greatest mystery. To think that I live on in my children is something I can't even comprehend. That if we look deep into our children's eyes, we can see our immortality!

All of the fathers interviewed wanted very much to have ongoing relationships—friendships actually—with their children when the children grew up. Some fathers were apprehensive about handling the teen years, when they themselves would be old. But others seemed philosophical.

All of the fathers to whom I spoke gave high recommendations to older parenting. Was it as bad as they'd feared? No, they said. Would they recommend it? Absolutely. Do they have any advice? Some.

"Just tell them to relax. Take it one day at a time," said Alvin. But Elliott did have a few words of caution.

Make sure you're ready. You can't just leap in without thinking about it. Look at all the kids today who don't have fathers. This can't be a whim. It's got to be a realized, mature decision.

Pat, rushing to get back to work, stopped at the door and turned back to tell me, "Yeah, I do have some advice —tell 'em to be prepared for a *wonderful* experience!"

Part IV

The Mother's Side

"Mothers are, and are not made."
—*George Middleton*

Chapter 18

The Grandparental Attitude

While I sat on a bench in a playground watching my daughter Elizabeth on a swing one Saturday, an elderly woman standing nearby turned to me and asked how old my granddaughter was. Naturally I was taken aback. I know she made a natural assumption but I didn't relate to it. Or to be more honest, I didn't *want* to relate to it. But, of course, the woman's idea was quite within the realm of possibility. I am indeed old enough to be a grandmother.

Instead, I am part of the new rising phenomena of late motherhood. However, mothers aren't the only ones who've undergone a transformation lately. Grandmothers, it seems, aren't what they used to be either. While mothers were once all in their twenties when they had their babies (with rare exceptions), mothers' ages now climb up into the late forties. Some women become grandmothers in their early forties, just when some of us are giving birth for the first time. Others become grandmothers in their sixties or even seventies. Grandmothers look so good these days it's hard to know who's the senior citizen and who's the senior in high school. *My* grandmothers certainly didn't do aerobics or run marathons. Grandmothers today have active social lives and hardly any time to just stay at home and bake for family gatherings. But whether or not a grandmother comes in a size 22 or a size 6, aerobically fit or not, she does come endowed with a special affection for her offspring. Grandmothers seem to love without the restraints parents often have, perhaps because they are not the primary caregiver any longer and don't carry the burden of responsibility parents carry. They appear to give affection freely and to deal with children on their level. I find it touching to hear adults comment on how remarkable their own relationships with their grandparents were.

Ironically, while interviewing one of the doctors for his medical expertise for this book, he began to talk about his special relationship with his grandfather.

When I look back on my childhood, my parents had very meager means and they both had to work. But I remember spending days and days with my grandfather. He was in his sixties and was the most wonderful person in my life. And still is. His knowledge and his patience to sit there and talk to a six-year-old boy and play with my mind—I don't think a twenty-five-year-old father can do that. When you're young you've got other issues.

I knew exactly what he was talking about. My husband exhibits what one mother calls a "Grandparental Attitude". What some of us are doing with our kids is a cross between standard parenting and grandparenting. It may appear to the outside world that we are more indulgent with these kids, but I've never heard anyone accuse a grandparent of over-indulging their offspring. Isn't that not only the grandparents' *job* but their right as well?

Our G.P.A. (Grandparental Attitude) is, without a doubt, one of the strongest delineators between younger and older parents. What accounts for this? Without a doubt, our age. Our maturity too. The affection grandparents feel for their grandkids is no doubt in part due to the natural mellowing and philosophical wisdom that occurs with age. And so if we *parent* at the time we biologically could be *grandparenting*, perhaps this partially accounts for our different attitude and style of parenting.

Maturing is generally a slow, yet profound, process. It impacts every aspect of our lives, especially our attitude toward the cycle of life and our own thoughts about death and our immortality through future generations. Sometimes what we learn is so personal it's hard to articulate to others.

I remember once having a rather heated discussion with one of my stepdaughters. She wanted to take a trip and we didn't approve. We felt she was too young. She was upset. Her final argument was that the only real difference between us was that we had the money and she didn't.

I remember weakly defending our decision against that argument but I knew I wasn't managing to make my point clearly. Now I know why. The futile defense I was offering, i.e., what if the car breaks down, what if you get arrested, what if you get injured, etc., wasn't going to penetrate a teenager's passionate desire. She wanted to go. In my gut, I knew it wasn't a good idea. And my gut reaction was based on some thirty-seven years of experience. The difference between us wasn't money. It was maturity. And no teenager likes to hear that they aren't mature. After all, they are related to you. They know how foolish you can be.

The difference in maturity also usually applies to a twenty-five-year-old mother versus a forty-five-year-old mother. Those two people are usually light years apart in terms of life experience. Thinking back on my own youth, when I was twenty-five I was still in transition. I was just beginning to learn about accepting personal responsibility. I began to make my first real efforts towards a career. I was learning about making choices and going after goals. Had I had a baby in my mid-twenties, I would never have enjoyed the career I did or experienced the thrill of buying my own house. More significantly, I probably would have been divorced by now, primarily because the men I was dating were not good candidates for fatherhood. They were like me, self-centered and immature.

So for me, waiting was truly a blessing. My child has been spared the mistakes of my immaturity and I was spared the guilt of seeing the havoc that would have wrecked on her.

This is by no means a way of saying that many younger mothers aren't good parents. My mother was twenty-two when I was born and because of that we now have the great joy of being together as two grown women. We have the luxury of a long-term friendship. My daughter may not have that luxury. What I *am* saying is that in my own case, I am a better mother because I am an older mother. And I am not alone. Here's what Joanne told me:

If I had had my kids in my twenties I'd have been
negligent, no question about it. I was very
wrapped up in myself at that time and they would
have gotten in the way. I would have made a mar-
tyr out of myself over them.

This from a woman who appears to be a model mother! Francine felt differently. "Let's face it. Someone who's
waited this long to have a child has some level of
self-absorption."
Almost every single mother I spoke with said that their
age greatly enhanced their patience level. They also
spoke of the mature ability to give to another human being. As Betty reported,

Age definitely enhanced having a baby. You're infinitely more patient, willing to step aside for another because your own needs have been fulfilled
and you *want* to be able to give to another person.

Diane said, "I would have resented the necessary
commitments. I was probably too selfish to do it earlier."
Marg contributed, "You're more patient and understanding of the needs of a small child. Things may appear
trivial, but to a child they aren't."
Alice mentioned,

I think age enhances my mothering, because I'm
not as concerned with the little things. Older parents don't get wrapped up in the things you're
"supposed" to do. You don't make an issue out of
making the bed or brushing teeth.

When I asked my interviewees how their age

negatively affected their mothering, they almost unanimously agreed that they lacked either the energy or the stamina that parenting a child often requires. Despite this drawback some mothers felt they could still keep up with their young children. "We ride bikes, I play ball with him," Faith insisted. "I don't think there's anything I can't do with him."

Stacy told me, "I do lots of things with my kids. We ice-skate, roller skate. We swim together. I took my kids to Discover Zone and went through all the tunnels with them—they loved it."

Whether you actively participate in you child's activities or not should be your choice. My young mother was very athletic, but I didn't learn to ride a bike until I was eleven, so parental youth is not always a deciding factor in being involved in your child's activities. What's more vital is your love and devotion.

It may be true that I am indeed old enough to be a grandmother, and that sometimes may account for my over-indulgence of my daughter. I'll never know. The stars just didn't come together until one night in February 1985. And, in my case, that was when I was ready and I'm glad that was how it happened.

Chapter 19

We're *All* Working Mothers

If ever the pattern of motherhood was undefined, it is now. It seems that almost daily, or at the very least weekly, there is some article focusing in on the debate about stay-at-home moms versus working moms. Raging controversies are carried on, but the bottom line seems to be this: the women's liberation movement has changed the concept and goals of women. The true aim of the liberation movement has always been to allow each individual woman the opportunity to make her own choice as to whether she wished to be single, a home-based working mom, a full-fledged stay-at-home mom, a part-time working mom or a full-time working mother. Those are largely the options of the modern woman. In the cases of the mature mothers to whom I spoke, each had made a personal decision as to parenting, as well as how she would parent and what part work would play in her family's life. No decision was frivolous, though some were altered once the reality of mothering began.

It seems interesting to me that we have accepted without question the idea of dual career families and never stopped to examine how such a concept began. In truth we have an historical background to thank for how we came to this place in time (See Mary Francis Berry's *The Politics of Parenthood*). During wartime, women have taken over the running of many highly skilled jobs and had the benefit of government assisted daycare. The Lanham Act provided for, among other things, the construction of daycare facilities for women who worked for the war effort. With the war ended, opponents to these facilities claimed they were no longer necessary, and though there was strong opposition to this argument, they were closed. Those of us raised in postwar America were affected by a national movement to help reestablish men in the working place once they returned home from the war. Family values—working dad, cookie-baking mom, and cute kids—became the goal of postwar America.

It wasn't until the women's movement made equality and equal work for equal pay priorities that women as a group once again sought "to have it all" just like men. The older mothers who were interviewed for this book had all worked prior to having a baby. Many still do. Some, like me, chose a part-time situation. But every woman made a conscious decision about whether or not she would work after the birth of her child. Nancy said,

I was the primary breadwinner in the family when I had my first child, so I had to go back to work.

Plus it so happened that there was a boom in my industry that I was eager to take advantage of. When our second child was born, I went to work two days later. I was traveling back and forth from the office to home to breastfeed two to three times a day, forty minutes each way. When she was around six months old, though, I felt that she and I hadn't properly bonded. She was more attached to the housekeeper than she was to me. So I quit working for a few months and spent that time making the bonding work. It was essential for our relationship.

Joyce, a mother who owns her own business, said,

My mother had passed away while I was pregnant and I had taken time out for that, and then I had our son by C-section and was home for a while recovering. But I couldn't take any more time off. There were too many people dependent on me. Plus I am a very important part of our financial picture. I have to work. What I discovered is that Super Mom doesn't exist. I thought I could get someone to help and bring the baby to work. *Fool.* I tried it and it *didn't* work. I had talked to girlfriends who were faking it. They weren't being honest about how hard it was. I don't know if it was that period (about seven years ago) but I think people are being a lot more straightforward about it now. I even remember the cover of *Savvy* magazine at the time showing a woman in a business suit with a briefcase in one hand and a baby on one hip! I consider myself such a practical person but I was *so* impractical about how having a baby would effect my life. I had no idea how torn I was going to be. I could not see him without feeling I should be at work and I could not be at work without thinking I should be with him. It was terrible, terrible. I'm much better about it now, but then he's got a life. It started to get better when he was about four and was in nursery school and started to have friends. But I wasn't the only one. My husband was the oldest of six kids and he thought he'd be really adept at managing all this, but at the beginning he panicked too. He'd go to the store for diapers and disappear for three hours!

Every situation is unique. Roberta explained,

I took four months off after my baby was born, then went back to work. I don't know why I went back, to tell you the truth. I didn't *have* to and my husband was begging me to stop. He saw me being torn in a million directions. Finally, I realized that I was fed up with my business and that I wanted more time with my daughter, so last year (when she was seven years old) I quit.

This is what happened to Tammy, another mother:

My husband and I had decided that I would stay home for the first few years when our daughter was born. I had been a physical education instructor and went on a leave of absence. When our daughter was four, the school district forced me to make a decision. I wasn't willing to put her in daycare so I quit. I had difficulty with that because I loved what I did, but in teaching I'd seen too many kids that had been left alone or with housekeep-ers, and I didn't like the end product. I saw kids who had to fend for themselves and had to make some decisions that perhaps weren't wise. There was nobody there steering them away from the bad decisions and validating the good ones. I didn't want that for our daughter.

Sara said,

I never planned on being a stay-at-home mom; it just sort of evolved that way. But when my son started at a co-op nursery school, I got involved there. Now that he's in grammar school, I'm in-volved there as well. I keep thinking about going back to work—but this is my work for now.

Grace told me,

I had been working at home when I got my pres-ent job offer. My son was five weeks old. I knew it was necessary for me to work and this job offered benefits and security, so I took it. And things have worked out really well. I didn't know how I could have remained creative on a daily basis if I'd stayed home.

But not all women want to go to the workplace. One mother admitted,

I was very torn but I felt that if you were going to have children you had a certain debt to them, and part of that debt is to be there at their activities and to lend them support. I think if children don't feel that emotional support, it's very detrimental. My sister asks me, "What do you *do*?" What I *do* is try to make the best possible life for my children and raise them the best way I know how within an environment that is supportive. I think when I show up for one of my son's ballgames I'm saying, just by being there, that I care about you, and what you do is important to me, and I'm *there*.

Alicia, a mother who works out of her home, said,

When the choice is returning fifteen business calls or "fwimming like fwoggies" in the pool we *must* make the right choice. We absolutely must not loose sight of the fact that being a mother is the most important thing in the world. Our world's future hinges on happy, well-adjusted human beings and only quality time will ensure that.

Stephanie, who worked and then quit, reported,

I went back to work when my son was seven months old but quit when he was four. It was only a hard decision in that I knew that the work place was the only place where I could get my ego strokes and I knew I needed them. But it was basically a happy decision and I was lucky I was able to do that.

Further elaborating on the change in her life, Stephanie revealed,

Having children has absolutely changed my life. I was on the path where you just make and do and when I stopped the focus of my life became *relationships* instead of *tasks*. And you cannot have relationships as a focus without undergoing a lot of self-examination and learning. And in that respect, I'm totally grateful because I've had to come to grips with myself. If I hadn't had to, why would I have? I was happy. I was fine . . . going about staying busy—busy so I never had to be with myself.

As an actress and later a freelance writer, I was never working on a full-time basis anyway. But I was keenly aware that when our daughter was born I needed to be with her on a full-time basis, because I felt it was essential to her well-being. Until she was almost six years old, I did not feel any full-blown desire to work again. I did have some urges when she started nursery school but I used my energies at the school.

However, as she grew more independent, so did I. My solution was to work part-time. Even now I write in a room that has toys scattered about, with a little desk next to mine where she can do her homework. I am constantly interrupted by a plethora of things: *I need breakfast, my hair needs brushing, Barbie's wedding dress isn't where I put it, I can't make my bed, I want lunch, where's my sweater?* Often I am in a stop, start, stop pattern. I drop her at school, make a dentist appointment, run back to school with something she forgot, pick her up from school, take her to the birthday party, her swimming lesson, and on and on and on. I do everything stay-at-home mothers do. And I write. Because for me I need the balance in my life. It was essential that I have a creative outlet, but one that was *not* more important than being at home in the morning, getting my child ready for school and picking her up when school is out. However, I do not have a financial need to work. So I could compromise; fitting my fulfillment needs around her schedule. And as she gets older I can take a bit more time for myself to do what I want. Right now she's watching a Disney video. I'm not reading to her, playing a game, or any other thing I could be doing with her; instead, I'm working. So I do play mouse games and Barbie occasionally, and I suffer guilt the rest of the time because I am not as perfect a mother as I'd like to be. Each of us has to find out what is needed and what works for us. Being mature, I believe, helps in making this decision.

I know that I am influenced by the era in which I grew up. I liked coming home to a house with a mother in it. I want my daughter to have the same sense of security I did. But I am also influenced by my past life experiences, by all that I've read and seen. This has led me to the way I have chosen to raise my daughter. I asked Bonnie why she thought some of us stayed home and some chose to go back to work. Here's what she said.

> Most of the time I think women make an unconscious choice about it. It really has to do with how you want to mother. I think there are degrees of mothering and some people want to do it on level B and some people want to do it on level A. It's really a matter of how down and dirty you want to get with this whole thing because it's kind of scary. Maybe some people just don't trust themselves to do it on level A. It's a huge responsibility and it's so evocative of so much emotional material. So if you don't want to do it that way you don't have to. I had no idea when I became a mother that it would be this hard.

Irene expressed another view, the fact that many working mothers work from necessity.

Our child was eagerly awaited by both of us. However, my husband is a free lance writer. For him it is feast or famine. However, to pay our bills we need a regular paycheck. As a computer programmer I provide that stability. So we never had any choice as to whether I would stay home or work. We both share parenting our little girl and I think that has many benefits.

Connie put it this way:

The choice my husband and I made was for me to be home, because we both felt that nobody would do it better than me. With some people their needs come first, while I think our children should come first. But I think our society is too divided when it comes to working versus stay-at-home mothers. I've seen some very unhappy mothers who are at home that shouldn't be. They're unhappy and that unhappiness permeates the home. So that's not good either.

One of the unfortunate things that seems to be going on these days is that women seem to feel sensitively about whatever lifestyle choice they have made when it comes to raising their children. If you are a full time stay-at-home mom you are sensitive to the criticism that you are not in the workplace, setting an example for your children, financially contributing to the family, raising independent children, and so on and so forth. If you are a working mother, you are raising children that do not have enough of your attention, you have chosen your needs over your child's, you're not always available for extracurricular activities, or you've handed your mothering role to someone else. We can't seem to win. But worst of all we are unsupported by society and so we feel very much alone on our journey. Role models are few and far between.

Ultimately I think things will be better. I hope my daughter will feel comfortable choosing her *own* way. Those of us who grew up in the 1950s still think wistfully of the television stereotypes of perfect mothers, when life seemed simpler and roles were defined. We long for the comfort of knowing that everyone is mothering the same way. But wasn't that perhaps movie hype? So many people I know grew up in dysfunctional homes, it's hard to find someone who had a "normal" childhood. And those childhoods all happened in the 1950s, so things weren't as tranquil as they seemed. Jackie summed it up best when she told me,

> My next door neighbor is a stay-at-home Mom and I always envied her her life. She gardens, cooks fabulous meals, goes to the gym, always looks good. But just last week she said she watches *me*—I have to work and am a full-time working mom and she is jealous of *my* situation. She thinks my life is exciting and glamorous—that I travel, have my own business, etc. We had a good laugh over *those* misconceptions. I figure God put us here, living right next to each other, so that we could learn from one another. I always think the grass is greener on the other side. But then, so does she!

Chapter 19

Women feel strongly about their parenting choices because nothing is more precious to mothers than their children. So when you criticize a choice someone has made you strike a deep, personal chord. Let's face it, parenting in general is changing and therefore we are all forging new ground. I never thought of myself as a pioneer, but in a sense we all are. We just need to remember that those who espouse a different style of parenting aren't enemies. We're in this together. And side by side, your child and mine will someday be left together in this world to run it.

Chapter 20

Second-Time Mothers

Love may be lovelier the second time around, but is motherhood? For those women who packed away the tiny undershirts and rattles, what motivates them to begin anew? What is the experience like for the woman who may still be married to the same man but chooses to have another child, the logistics of which may mean a big spread in years between two children? While many of us past thirty-five years of age thrill at the notion of having a first child, for someone who knows what lies ahead, the commitment to a new baby can appear either daunting or delicious. Said Veronica:

> My husband mentioned the idea to me one morn-
> ing totally out of the blue, and I just thought it was

so romantic. I forgot all of the negatives and just thought it sounded splendid for all of us—fun and sweet and all that.

In that romantic state, this mother went on to have her third child. When her baby was born she already had an eleven-year-old and a fourteen-year-old.

There is a seven-and-a-half-year age spread between my younger brother and me. Though my mother was still quite young when she had him, she says that what she essentially did was have two only children. When my brother was a newborn, I was at school all day. While he was still in grade school, I left for college. Though we were very much a family, that time spread meant we experienced a different set of parents. Their experiences and maturity with parenting and life in general gave them a different point of view with each of us. The same people were our parents, but our parents weren't the same people.

I spoke with women, the majority of whom were in their second marriages, and asked what second-time mothering after a long hiatus was like. Here's what some of them said.

Alice told me:

My present husband had never had children. I had two kids from a previous marriage. They were already teenagers. My husband wasn't sure if he wanted to have a child or not, so I gave him a time limit because I knew I was getting up there. As it turned out, I had my son when I was thirty-nine. I was scared—maybe *panicked* is a better word, because I knew what was in store. I kept thinking, *Can I face* Mommy and Me *again?*

I asked Alice how she did face what lay ahead. She explained:

Luckily I had a few friends who were going through the same thing at the same time. Another woman and I went to the director of *Mommy and Me* and told her, "Look, we want to do this, but you've got to find us some older mothers." And she did. She found three other mothers, some of whom were on their second marriages.

I asked Alice why she wanted a group with older mothers.

Older mothers aren't as concerned about little things. Our questions were "How are we going to get through this period of our lives?" Even though we loved these children dearly, it was tough. My friend had a Ph.D. in anthropology and I had an MBA. We'd done all these accomplished things, and here we were stuck changing diapers at forty years of age. I thought, *I'm gonna go crazy.* On top of that, my friend wound up having twins, and one had a learning disability. It was a lot to get through.

Did the group of older mothers help?

We all stuck together and even had a play group with the kids that lasted until they all got into kindergarten. It was great. we would sit at the park with our toddlers and discuss our problems with our teenagers. Our *Mommy and Me* was really *Mommy and Me and Teenagers.* I discovered that a two-year-old and a teenager behave very similarly.

Beth, another mother who also had teenagers, concurred:

> I'd say it's very hard to have teenagers and a baby. It's hard to juggle all that. I didn't know how hard it would be to juggle work, kids, and time. I love the baby, but the routine has been *so* difficult.

Mary told me how she was different as a mother this time as compared to her first mothering experience.

> When I had my first child, I was very career oriented. I was in my thirties and very driven. The first child just happened. When it happened I wanted her, but this child was a love child. It makes a big difference. Both my husbands were at the deliveries, but my first husband couldn't handle it. My second husband was wonderful. So even though both the deliveries were tough, I think the second one was easier because I'd been through it before, and that helped.

Dara told me what kind of mother she was the second time around:

> With my other child I was a single mom and had to work and go to school, so there was no time together, This new child has a much more traditional family life. It's entirely different. For one thing, he has a dad living with him and I'm home all the time.

Connie said:

I have a much better sense of humor about everything. When I was younger I thought I was going to be the perfect mother, and I held myself to that far too rigidly. "She will be read to every night," "She will not eat sugar"—you know, those kinds of rules. Now we go with the flow. I'm much more relaxed.

Gerrie told me:

I'm about the same, actually. I'm maybe not as attentive because I have more work and more children.

Samantha put it this way:

I'm still making the same mistakes. Sometimes I think I may even worry *more* now, believe it or not. I'm actually less cool and more clingy in some ways. I'm aware this time it isn't going to last.

All is not bliss. Here's what Fran had to say:

Because I'm older I'm more anxious for time for me, and that's hard. With the others I felt I had my whole young life ahead of me, but with this one it's like, "Hurry and grow up so I have time to read, to play the piano, to sit and think—whatever."

This is an issue for many older mothers. We are aware that there is little time for selfish pursuits. For a mother who saw an end to her mothering years with her older children, beginning again means a great sacrifice. The postponement of freedom, which appeared so close at hand, may be difficult.

Perhaps there is some benefit to having older children in the house. Doesn't having a teenager in the house provide you with a built-in babysitter?

> Only if she's paid. I have to book her in advance.

> Are you kidding? They're never home.

> Both my kids are off at college.

> My daughter is in college, and my son is in his senior year and is heavy into sports, so he's never home.

> I wouldn't trust him. It's not that he'd hurt the baby; he just doesn't have an instinct for kids.

So much for the advantages to having a teenager and a baby at the same time. Unfortunately, older children with busy social lives are often not available for their siblings the way a child closer in age may be.

If the older mothers I interviewed seemed more relaxed in general, how much more relaxed were the mothers who had been through it all before? While we novices fret, they flash understanding grins. Shirley explained why:

> I think I'm less worried about certain things— schools, for example. I have some perspective. I see that the "right" school isn't what makes a child happy or successful.

For those of us who are doing parenting for the first and possibly only time, our choices have overwhelming importance. Because most of us have only the one child, there is not the chance to make up for our mistakes down the line. There aren't four other children with whom to iron the kinks out. My father says, "Children should be like pancakes: the first one should just be for practice." We older mothers don't have that luxury.

The second-time mothers with whom I spoke seemed infinitely more secure in their roles. They have faced what the rest of us fear—namely, the teenage years. They came to motherhood even more conscientious because they fused age and experience. Of all the children who are the products of older mothers, these may indeed be the most interesting to track. Motherhood, it seems, *is* lovelier the second time around.

Chapter 21

Single Motherhood

In the past, being an older single mother was an eye-raising situation. The only *respectable* single mother was a widow. The words *older, single,* and *mother* were never used in the same sentence. A single mother was persona non grata. Who would ever risk such a thing? Today's women, that's who.

The television character Murphy Brown may be more successful in business than the average older single mother, but in many ways she is similar. She made a choice to be a mother, even though it meant doing it on her own. The single mothers I interviewed for this book were among the most interesting people I have ever met. Each was as unique as the route they chose to motherhood. They saw themselves as neither gutsy nor daring.

They simply did what they felt was right—they followed their hearts.

Single motherhood was something I had contemplated before meeting my husband. For personal reasons, I rejected that route, but the single mothers I spoke with voiced a sentiment I had experienced: Why should the lack of a mate deny one the chance to fulfill one of the most important desires a woman may have? For some being pushed into a corner by their biological clock, it meant a now-or-never decision. Some discovered they were pregnant while in the midst of a divorce or breakup. Motherhood could no longer be pushed to the future. The future had arrived, and the decision was at hand.

Within the last ten years there has been a 56 percent increase in the number of unmarried mothers in the eighteen-to-forty-four age bracket. The women within this age group made the decision to have a child for a wide variety of reasons. On one hand there is the high school student, and on the other the mature business executive. While both may be single mothers, their experiences and the experiences of their children are light years apart. Once ridiculed and shunned as bastards, children of older single mother today have generally the same societal advantages as other children in their economic group. While it is true that we still operate as a family-oriented society, we have nonetheless become increasingly accustomed to new kinds of families. Out-of-wedlock births have never occurred so openly and with so few eyebrows being raised.

One factor in this trend is that adoption, a popular choice among older single mothers, is an option. Until recently, adoption was generally unavailable to single parents, who had to travel to other countries or accept children with serious medical conditions to fulfill their parenting desires. These women's single status wasn't the only hurdle they had to overcome. Age limits were placed on couples wishing to adopt as well. Being over thirty-five gave a woman a second strike against her.

Similarly, breakthroughs in medical science have provided older single mothers with assistance with many correctable infertility problems and even artificial insemination when desired. So more older single women are choosing to become pregnant.

Ironically, Candice Bergen, who plays the character Murphy Brown, has become the banner carrier of the single mother movement, yet in real life she gave birth to her daughter in a traditional home. She remains married to director Louis Malle, but to thousands her character's choice to parent alone gave voice to what many knew was happening all around the world. Single women were choosing to bear and raise their children with or without fathers.

One reason women may choose to become single mothers is that they never find the right man. Jeanne told me:

> I had been engaged three different times. I'd always promised myself that someday I'd have a baby. I was thirty-four when I broke up with the last guy, and I'd always promised myself when I was in my twenties that if I hit thirty-five and wasn't married, I'd have a baby. So when we broke up, I said, "That's it. I want a home, and what if I wait and then can't have a child?" I could envision never getting married, but never having a child was something I couldn't bear.

Lauren said:

I had been married for quite a few years, and we had actively tried to have a baby. In fact, the constant trying put a big strain on our marriage. Another big strain was that my husband had a child from a previous marriage who stayed with us during the summer and for holidays. My husband refused to discipline her and wouldn't allow me to discipline her either. Consequently there were wet towels on the floor, food all over the room—it was awful. One day I realized I didn't *like* the way he parented, and I realized I didn't want to have a child with him. So after some extensive therapy, I told him I was leaving, which I did. After a year I began the adoption proceedings.

Maureen explained:

Most of my friends were getting married and settling down because they knew that if they didn't they wouldn't have a child. So they found someone decent and said, "Okay." Now they have kids and it's not like they're miserable, but they're not that happy either. Luckily I had inherited some money, so I had the luxury of being able to do it on my own.

Gail told me:

I didn't want to have a man just to have a baby. That seemed selfish. You know, women in the past have always needed men to have babies, and I think it scares a lot of men that maybe we don't need them anymore. But now there is the social acceptance that a single mother is okay. Besides, many of the men I was meeting were either older, had had vasectomies, or had already had kids and didn't want any more.

Naturally, as women get older the men they date get older as well. Gail described what I heard from many women. It takes a certain amount of serendipity for an older woman wishing to be a mother and a man wishing to be a father to come together, Many women claim their dating takes on a different tone when they approach age thirty-five. For some the search for a man to father their child becomes frantic. Melanie said:

I didn't see the individual I was dating anymore. I saw a potential father. After a while I knew I wasn't giving these guys a fair shake, so I decided to just have the baby. To hell with waiting for Mr. Right. What if he never shows up and I had missed out on the joys of being a mom and of having my own family?

Kristy told me:

I had been married for a long time and we kept putting off having a baby, basically because my doctor told me I didn't have to worry about it until I was thirty-eight. So I waited, and then I couldn't get pregnant. After I was divorced I dated and couldn't find that someone special but knew I still wanted a child. One day I ran into a girlfriend who was so matter-of-fact about her decision to become a single mother that I thought, *I'll do it.* So I decided to adopt. My only regret now is that I gave up my primary childbearing years and couldn't have a biological child. By not having given birth I feel somehow as though I didn't fulfill that cycle. Ironically, there's a woman who sits next to me at work who's nine months pregnant and is always complaining about how uncomfortable she is, and I have to bite my tongue because I'd have given anything to go through that discomfort.

As many women begin to take charge of their own lives, it is inevitable that some will begin to make untraditional choices. Women in general are breaking new ground. Single women are breaking new ground altogether.

Many years ago Marlo Thomas wrote a book and produced a television show entitled "Free to Be a Family." The premise was that there are many ways to make a family. It needn't be Mom, Dad, Baby, and the white picket fence. While many may still choose that route, I hope we are liberal enough to embrace all forms of families. For these single moms, they are free enough to be a family of two.

The biggest concern that the single mothers I spoke with have is without a doubt the lack of a father in their children's lives. All the mothers are aware that it is a serious issue. Eileen told me:

The hardest part of being a single mother is that my child will grow up without a father. I have a problem with that. She sees a mommy and a child on "Sesame Street" and they say on television that that's a family, so thank goodness she hears it, but I still have a problem with it. And even though she's adopted, it would be no different if her father and I were divorced. I'd still feel badly that she didn't have a father around. There's certainly much more social acceptance now, but some questions that strangers ask me are hard to answer, like "Oh, she must look like her father," or "Where does she get her blue eyes?" I tell them, "From God."

Admittedly this was my personal stumbling block when I thought about single parenting. I felt strongly that a child needed both parents and gambled that I still had a couple years left to find a mate. I was lucky, but I often wonder what I would have done if I'd been the age these women were when they made their choices. Sara was one who discovered she was pregnant while going through a divorce.

I feel very badly for my son because his father has never even seen him and probably never will. And it took years of therapy before my son was old enough to be able to identify and express some of his pain over that.

Barb told me:

I have a man in my life who is very devoted to both of us. My daughter loves him very much and wants to call him Daddy, and he wants her to. There is a good possibility that one day we'll marry, but if we were to break up he would still be her daddy. Even if I were to marry someone else, I would maintain that relationship between the two of them.

In an effort to provide her child with a father figure, Barb may be opening herself up to a potentially hazardous situation. If the relationship with this man does end, he may have legal grounds for gaining custody of the child. Already, an unmarried man in California—in fact, an openly gay man—with no biological link to the child and who was never married to the child's mother, had recently gained custody of the child who calls him Daddy. The court upheld that his active participation as the child's father gave him the legal status of that role.

Some of the mothers I interviewed preferred having no man participate in parenting their child. While they understood the importance of a male influence, they did not want "interference." For this reason Helen chose artificial insemination. Helen told me:

> I chose a sperm bank because I didn't want complications. I didn't want some guy coming back and saying, "I don't want you moving out of state," "I don't want my kid living here," "I don't want my kid going to this school," et cetera, et cetera. I have some girlfriends whose men had said, "Okay, it's your child, you can have it, I won't interfere." And then as soon as the baby was born they were all over the place, and I didn't want that.

Nancy said:

> While it might be nice to have someone to help every now and then, I like that I can decide what's best for my child. I don't have to do battle with someone else.

But while all these women choose to parent alone,

they were not without a support system to see them through. For most of the women I spoke with, that support system was their family. Claire told me:

My mother, believe it or not, went with me to the sperm bank to pick up the sperm and then came with me to the gynecologist. Needless to say she's been very supportive.

Peggy explained:

My family and I have always been very close. My parents live in this wonderful apartment building, and they were always saying, "You should move in upstairs." But I thought that would be too close. When the baby was born my mother moved in for what I thought would be a couple days, and after three weeks, when my dad was anxious for her to come back home, I said, "I'm ready to move in upstairs," and it's been great. Every evening after dinner my daughter goes downstairs for an hour. If I want to shower, they'll watch her. If I have a date, they'll watch her. The only downside is finding a man that likes my family as much as I do. The guy I'm dating now does, thank goodness.

Some women aren't as lucky as this woman. Carrie said:

I have to pay for my support system. I pay for a nanny, a housekeeper, a shrink, a coach—you name it. And even though my family is very supportive, they live some distance away. And when they're here the good times only last for a few days. Then it turns into a not-so-healthy atmosphere and I sometimes have to call an end to the visit.

Emotional support isn't the only kind these single mothers need to worry about. Without the benefit of a husband and father to help with the finances, these women take on a heavy load. April told me:

> If my father hadn't left me with a nice inheritance, I couldn't have done this, so he really made having my daughter possible. I was a second grade teacher before all this happened, and there's no way I would have had a child just to leave her in daycare all day. I couldn't have handled that. It would have seemed too selfish.

Vicki said:

> I've had it pretty cushy. I was working as a lawyer, and even though the hours were pretty good I was only home with her in the evenings. So for a year I thought every day about leaving my job, and thank God my parents gave me the emotional support to do it. They said it was okay. And now I'm working part-time, and since these are such important times with her, I'm happy to have it. I love taking her to the park.

Tammy explained:

> When I adopted my daughter my career was going very well, and I assumed that would continue. But in the last few years I've hit a real slump. In

essence I have to start all over in a new line of work because I don't think the business I was in is going to provide the kind of security I want. This would have happened to me with or without a child, but now that I am our sole support, it feels like more of a responsibility than it felt before.

Cecille told me:

I feel the pressure more, sure, but I also have a *reason* to be working so hard. There's someone I am working hard for and someone that makes it all worthwhile.

Jane said:

The women who have a hard time as single mothers are the ones who have economic hardships. If you don't have a job that will give you enough money to pay the rent *and* provide a housekeeper, then you'll really go crazy, because then you have no relief. I've seen single mothers who have moved in together and split the rent and the childcare, and that seems to be the only alternative. But luckily the older women I know who've been single and had children had some economic security.

As with most older mothers, these women who embarked on single motherhood generally had some level of career security. Having spent the last twenty years building a career, most of these women had reaped the economic rewards of their hard work—homes or condos, cars, medical insurance. These women were used to shouldering responsibilities. They were willing to take on a new commitment. At least from an economic standpoint, parenthood was not daunting to these older mothers.

But not every woman came to single motherhood solely by choice. When I interviewed Toni, this was her story:

> I had been married for seven years and helped raise my husband's two kids from a previous marriage. When I was six months pregnant, I developed spinal meningitis, which put me into the hospital. It was quite a time. I had three groups of doctors checking in on me at one time—the ones for meningitis, my OB, and the neo-natalogists. One day they were prepping me for a spinal tap and the neo-natalogist was telling me they didn't know how all of this might be affecting my baby. Just then my husband arrived with some of my things from home and told me he was leaving me. I was completely stunned. My head was reeling. How I got through that time I'll never know. So even though I am a single mother—am *delighted* to be a mother—it was not a conscious choice on my part to embark on this alone.

One of the toughest aspects of single motherhood is the sense of isolation it can sometimes bring. That sense of isolation can be very tough. Mona related:

> People tend to forget you when you're not part of a couple. You don't get invited out a whole lot, mainly I think because if you're friendly with the wife, who's the husband going to talk with while

the hamburgers are on the grill? On the other hand, if you know the husband and not the wife, that's not too comfortable. If there are other couples at a get-together it's no easier because you're the odd man out, so people just overlook you.

Norma said:

It seems that when my daughter was born a lot of people pushed me away. I hadn't told many people that I was going to adopt because I didn't want to have to go back to everyone if it didn't work out, and that made some friends feel left out. So I have fewer friends now.

In a world of couples, single parent often need to find one another to gain the kind of support they need. Various groups have sprung up all over the country. One group that is specifically geared to the needs of single mothers is called Single Mothers By Choice (212-988-0993). They provide a network that is helpful for single mothers of all ages. But Terry, one middle-aged mom, told me that she doesn't go to as many gatherings as she used to:

I really didn't want to hear about a super line of toys that someone was excited about. Lately I'm interested in having a will drawn up and thought, as fellow single mothers who are solely responsible for their children, that this would be a hot topic. But only the older mothers seemed interested.

Some of the single mothers said they didn't feel they were "group" material, while others expressed real interest in getting together with others in similar circumstances.

All these older mothers reported the same fatigue that many mothers had complained about. To varying degrees some women missed having someone else with whom to parent. Mona summed it up this way:

> I have no one to bounce my decisions off of. It's me alone, and it's hard to know all the time if I'm doing the right thing.

She then proceeded to give me an interesting example:

> For a long time I felt so badly that my son was growing up without a father that I tried to be both mother and father to him. That included rough-housing (and resulted in me breaking my arm one time) and participating in what I refer to as "male games"—you know, making rude sounds, et cetera. Since I've always been something of a tomboy, it was easy for me to slip into these games. A few months ago, however, a couple of good friends took me aside and said it was getting out of hand. My son didn't know when to stop. Playing all those games is something fathers do with their sons, they reminded me, but mothers teach them when it's gone overboard. Mothers refine their sons, and what I had to learn was that I can only be a mother to my son, and that's going to have to be enough.

I asked these mothers how they felt about mothering. Would they do it again? Said Keira:

From the day I brought my daughter home, my life has changed completely—and so much so for the better, I can't believe it. My life is fuller.

Dana said:

My son is the best thing in my life. You know, sometimes I run into a woman who asks me how old my son is, and when I tell her he's almost eight she'll say, "Oh, I could never go through that again. Thank God it's you and not me." And I think that says so much about what she thought of her parenting experience. I can guarantee one thing: Despite all the craziness that I've gone through in the last nine years, you will never hear me say that about my parenting time. I escape all the madness in the world just to be with him. He is the joy of my life.

Alex had this opinion:

She is my whole life. I know I should date, but I want her to be my main focus. I never for one minute take my daughter for granted. It's like when I went to graduate school. I paid for it, so I worked very hard and got terrific grades. Well, that's the way it is with my daughter. I wanted her very badly, and I never forgot how special she is to me.

But not all mothers were thrilled with the entire package. Teddie told me:

I was pretty taken aback by motherhood. If you

didn't spend a lot of time with kids when you were younger you are totally unprepared. Motherhood on a daily, hourly basis is overwhelming. It's not like a boyfriend; this is forever. There's a dark side to motherhood that no one wants to talk about. We've all been brainwashed by television. Everything on television is happy and cozy. So when the tough times come, you're not ready for it. I was talking to a friend one day—she doesn't have any kids, by the way—on a day when the baby had been screaming for four hours straight, and I told my friend I wanted to kill her. She was appalled and said, "She's only a baby!" Like I was crazy, which I was at the time. There's also a competitive thing that goes on with some people: "Your baby isn't sleeping through the night yet?" "Your baby isn't crawling?" That kind of thing. That's been interesting.

What else did the other older moms consider important? Carrie said:

A male influence is important, but not necessarily a husband. The younger single mothers seem a bit more interested in that. The older mother wants her children included in her dating, too. Not all the time, but I don't think we care about going out a lot, especially since most of us work and have so little time with our kids as it is. It's hard to take time away from your child to go and have dinner with someone you barely know. I didn't have a child to leave her alone.

Jayne related this story:

A man I'd been dating was at my house late one night and we were watching television. My seven-year-old woke up with a bad case of leg cramps, and I went to soothe him for a few minutes. When I came back this man I had thought was so nice had his coat on and was at the front door. He didn't want to share me with a child, and frankly I didn't want a man that couldn't understand the difference.

My first reaction when I heard Jayne's story was "How sad." Then I recalled my own dating years and remembered how it sometimes takes a long time to find out some people's real worth. If you are a woman who has chosen to have a child without a man, then it would seem that any man who enters the picture later is going to have to accept your parenting as a part of who you are.

Genevieve told me this to illustrate just how much her life has changed:

Before I had my child I was a freelance writer living on a boat. When I decided to have a child, I went to school to become a paralegal, bought a condo, and now have this wonderful life. It's not that I miss the freedom or the boat or the way of life. I don't. My life has changed so completely for the better I can't believe it. My life is richer now. Someday I may do all that again, but for now my needs are completely different. I'm happy to stay at home and be with my daughter. I'm dedicated to being with her. You know, on the weekend I get into the pool with her and we play. I see these younger mothers, whose kids are in the water, sitting there sunbathing. They don't spend any time with their kids, and I spend the whole time with her. It makes you wonder. Maybe they don't want to get their hair wet. I don't care about getting my hair wet; I care about being with my daughter.

Like their married counterparts, the effort older single moms expended on having their children makes these children especially precious and loved. Being raised in a society that is now open to various forms of families will help both these mothers and their children to feel more secure in the roles they have chosen.

It appears from the growing numbers that single motherhood is not a passing fancy. As medical science continues to enhance our ability to mother at increasingly advanced ages, coupled with wider guidelines for adoption, there will be even more older single mothers. What a miracle that being single no longer dooms a woman to perpetual "aunthood." How incredible that women who always felt in their hearts that they were meant to be mothers can. How remarkable that we live in a society that has made the leap to embrace a wider interpretation of the family. How wonderful that these single women are free to be a family—a family of two.

Chapter 22

Advice, *Madre a Madre*

Without a doubt, things change when you bring a child into your life. The old status quo needs a major overhaul, that's for sure. Here is a list of things that older mothers advise other women to do once they have had children. There's nothing profound here, just tips from those who've been in the trenches. It's an eclectic grouping to be sure, but perhaps some of these ideas will help you along the way.

    1. Give Up. Accept that there is no way you can handle all that you used to do. Just realize that lots of things are going to be done poorly compared to your old standards—if they get done at all. Don't worry; it won't last forever—only about twenty-five years.

2. Reprioritize. Unless something is absolutely neces-sary, especially when you have a small baby, get rid of it. Know that you can't accommodate anything but the es-sentials when a baby is young. Forgive yourself for this. One mother I know summed it up when she told this story: She had had her second baby within fourteen months of the first and was well over thirty-five. When someone came to the door, she answered it in her robe, which she claims to have been in for three days, and said, "If you're not here to help, leave." And she meant it. One year my New Year's resolution was to wash my face every night before I went to bed. When I say essential, I mean *essential.*

3. Rent Movies. Checking out the latest foreign film at a romantic little theater is a thing of the past and a pursuit only for the distant future. It's just as exciting waiting to see what's being released this month at your local video store.

4. Socialize with the Parents of Your Child's Friends. A sure-fire way to ruin any social get-together is to have your Suzy and their Billy biting and crying. Or worse: to have your single friend's Waterford bowl smashed to the floor by your curious two-year-old. Conversely, barbecuing at a house where the grownups can talk and the kids can also have a good time makes for a relaxing and enjoyable get-together.

5. Limit Your Contact with Childless Couples Unless They Are Good Friends. People who don't have kids go crazy when Wendy throws up on their new carpet. They also don't know why you don't just get a long list of reli-able babysitters (proving once again that they don't under-stand the problem) or if you do and your child has a fever why you don't feel comfortable leaving her and going out. Only *good* single friends can bear with you while you're learning the ropes. Bless them that they will also feed you a meal that isn't cut into bite-size pieces.

6. When Your Child Is Acting Up. If you're out in public, claim they're your grandkids and let it be known you don't approve of the way your daughter is bringing them up. This is one time when age lines come in handy.

7. Use the Kids as an Excuse. It's terrific for declining those invitations you'd otherwise have to accept. The line is "We'd love to, but you know how it is—we're asleep by eight o'clock." Who wants people falling asleep at their dinner table?

8. Accept Change. It is very difficult for women who have spent thirty-five years or more organizing to get used to chaos, but you just have to. On first observance, I thought the first- and second-grade teachers at my daughter's school were rather casual regarding the clutter on their desks. I thought to myself, "I'd go nuts if I had a desk with forty million things piled over it." Then one day while I was cleaning out my daughter's messy shelves, I realized, "But of course, she's got this kind of mess dumped on her by a whole classroom of kids." After that I was amazed that these teachers remained so good-natured and got so much accomplished. The school room *could* be immaculate, but that would also indicate a personality trait that may not be as relaxed around kids—or as much fun.

9. Make Friends. As soon as humanly possible, look for some kind of support group, but not necessarily one with *Anonymous* in the name. Try Mommy and Me, Gymboree, Tadpole Swimmers—anything. These groups are formed not for the children's sake but to give the mothers a legitimate place to meet and talk. Let's face it: few babies ever learn to do the backstroke or walk a balance beam. I'm convinced the real purpose is to give mothers the chance to mingle with others in the same boat. By the way, it's easy to spot other older mothers—they're reading *Lear's*.

10. Speaking of Reading. Unless it's something to do with child development or a magazine article entitled "How to Get the Sizzle Back in Your Sex Life," you won't be reading much until the first grade—unless you count *Goodnight Moon* (which I do).

11. Choose Hotels Wisely. The only way to survive any family vacation is in a hotel or motel that has a mini-refrigerator at least. Young children do not have the patience for room service or the time it takes to get everyone dressed and to a restaurant. They often wake up starving and thirsty. Some hotels even have microwave ovens, which is even better. If you can afford a suite, they also enhance your enjoyment of the holiday. The extra room for the kids to play in, as well as separate sleeping accommodations, gives you a sense of freedom that would be impossible with them sleeping in the next bed. There are now a good number of hotel chains that are targeting families with lures like Kids Clubs and provide excellent service in all price ranges.

12. Go Away Alone. Many mothers stressed the importance of this to me, but frankly I found it very difficult to do. There aren't many people you can ask to watch a young child. Another consideration for me was the fact that our daughter was too young to be left, in my opinion, for the first few years. I didn't feel she would understand what was happening. Many mothers strongly disagree. You have to follow your heart, but we can't forget that eventually we're going to be left alone with our husbands. It's not a bad idea to see what that feels like occasionally.

13. Car Trips. For every hour that you're on the road, give a small toy. This is so helpful when you're taking any trip over an hour. Kids get bored and/or car sick, and this keeps them motivated to behave. They are also occupied for at least thirty seconds trying to figure out how the toy works and then can spend forty minutes telling you that it doesn't work. This fills the time.

14. Air Travel. Ask for outside bulkhead seats. You need to be on the aisle so you can walk the child around. The bulkhead is the first in the cabin and has some leg room. This is great for the diaper bag when they're little and is a good place for them to play when they're toddlers.

15. Restaurants. I now delight in going to restaurants that I wouldn't have considered ten years ago. Some are large chains that usually have waitresses in the same uniform across the United States. They usually look the same inside whether you're in Portland or Philadelphia. Don't berate them; they're great. They almost all have kiddie menus and often give out crayons to occupy kids until the food arrives. The child's menu is suitable to kids' tastes and, best of all, waitresses are not appalled by the mountain of crumbs, peas, and fries that wind up on the chairs and floor.

16. Check Out Discount Stores. It could be a Target, Wal-Mart, K-Mart, or any number of discount stores. These stores have great kids clothes and toys at really reasonable prices. Naturally if you can afford more, that's great, but most kids outgrow or outwear their clothes and toys in short order. Attractive, well-made clothes are available for a fraction of the cost. I'm saving the big bucks for the teen years, when I'll need to spend them.

17. Don't Forget Libraries. Or Librarians. While my daughter owns a mountain of books, she still loves new ones. Learning to read is helped by having a variety of different books to make the task more fun. Libraries are free resources, and the librarians have been most helpful in giving us some great reading suggestions.

18. Talk to Other Mothers. Especially older ones. If you don't join a group, at least seek out other older mothers. The emotional support is important, and other mothers' suggestions will help you through more than I could ever write about.

19. Remember: This Is a Phase. This is not your whole life, just a part of it. Enjoy it while you can. Small children quickly grow up. Someday, these will be the good old days, and you just may miss them.

Part V

The Spiritual Side

"Nature is a volume of which God is the author."
—*Moss Harvey*

Chapter 23

Exploring Another World

Though I expected to feel and experience love on a deeper level once we had our daughter, what I didn't expect was the overwhelming spiritual understanding that would begin to develop the first time I looked into my daughter's eyes.

I am a part of a generation that has undergone much experimentation with meditation, spirituality, and traditional religion. My own path began with Catholicism, ventured into New Age philosophy for a while, meandered into a moderate Christian congregation for a few years, and has now wound up with my believing that true spiritual growth is independent and private in nature. I believe that growth can take place in or out of a structured environment. At this stage I am not a part of any religious community. My spiritual path is being explored, at least for the time being, privately.

Our choice for our daughter is moderate. We chose a school for her that has an ecumenical overtone. While it is connected to an Episcopal church, the school is careful to celebrate all religious holidays so that exposure to different beliefs and cultures takes place at an early level. Our philosophy coincides with the school in that we believe that what you teach early stays. Hopefully learning a lack of prejudice for people, their cultures, and their religions will help develop her into the kind of human being we feel is needed in this world. We chose an environment that would introduce her to God in a gentle way. Ultimately I want her to choose to have God in her life or not. More importantly, I wanted her to hear from a very early age that there *is* a spiritual side to life. No matter what you choose to call it or how you wish to address it, it does exist.

Connecting to the spiritual side of life usually takes a bit of time. The energy of youth demands—generally speaking, at any rate—a self-absorption that allows little room for contemplating the unknown. The rush to begin a career, to find a mate—these things take an enormous amount of energy. When those tasks are completed and there is room to go within, the need to explore the spiritual sometimes begins.

In the United States it appears that religion is on the way back. As we return to more conventional family values and step away from the greed of the '80s, we begin to embrace old traditions. And religion is one of those traditions. While I eschewed religion as a single and even a married person, I am rethinking my position now that I have become a mother. I am going to profoundly affect another human being, and I wanted to make sure she is introduced to her spiritual side.

Before Elizabeth was born I was one of those people who believed that babies couldn't really see at birth. Not only did mine seem to see, but she peered at me for a long time when I first held her, as if to say, "Oh, so *you're* the one." She also would gaze deeply into her father's eyes for long stretches of time, which was mesmerizing. We thought she was unusual.

One of Elizabeth's favorite stories is about the day after she was born. I laid her on the bed and hobbled over to use the bathroom, dragging my IV the whole way. From the minute I put her down until I shuffled back and picked her up, she screamed her head off. The minute I picked her up, she sighed. She wasn't wet, she wasn't hungry. She wanted her mommy. Only if I was holding her would she stop crying—and that lasted for years! But what was significant about the act was that this day my baby was already connected. She knew what she wanted and who she wanted. During visiting hours they would take her back to the nursery, and the second time they did the nurse called to tell me my baby had woken the entire nursery and could I please ask my guests to leave so they could return her to me? Once in my arms, she would fall asleep. That's when I first began to believe in the spiritual side of life.

Our child was not the blank slate I had imagined a baby to be. She was not un*formed*. She was just un*known*—at least to me. The baby asleep in my arms seemed so serene and knowledgeable. I found myself thinking more about the afterlife—and the *before*life. And karma. I began looking at other babies and saw the vast differences between them. I observed how one three-year-old would be terrified of ants while another would call them "my pets." I noticed that while one loved to sing, another would have no interest in it. One was shy, another was extroverted. It wasn't *all* parental influence. There had to be more to it. My child became a catalyst to a deeper spiritual awareness. Ideas that had merely crossed my mind before now got quickly clarified. I believe that because I was older I had begun to ask the age-old question, "What is it all about?" And she was providing me with the answers.

Good friends told us a story about *their* good friends who were expecting their second child. Their little girl was fully informed and quite excited about the prospect of becoming a big sister. She was around four years old at the time and kept telling her parent, "When the baby is born, I want to be alone with it." She repeated this so often that the parents became a bit concerned. Was she really as excited about the birth as she claimed, they wondered, or was she merely covering some plan to do the baby harm? The baby was born and the request was repeated: "Remember, I want to be alone with the baby." The nervous parents consulted with their pediatrician, who suggested that they let her be alone with the baby but to put the baby monitor on so that if anything sounded strange they could intervene. So they did. As they sat nervously hunched over the baby monitor, they heard their daughter whisper to the baby, "Quick, remind me what it was like. I'm beginning to forget."

Once when Elizabeth was about three I was chopping her an egg and she said to me quite casually, "My other mommy didn't do it like that." "Oh?" I said, not trying to sound too startled but curious beyond measure, "How did your other mommy do it?" "Different" was her only answer. "What did your other mommy look like?" I asked. Now I was hooked. "Not as pretty as you," she said and turned to her flexi-blocks. It never came up again, but it made an impression. One mother told me her daughter described the "bright people" who sometimes came and talked to her. She was a bit startled but instructed her husband and son not to make fun of the child if she talked about them. "What if she really is seeing something the rest of us can't?"

When Elizabeth was seven, she told me she'd seen angels that day. "Oh, where?" I casually asked. "In chapel." I was mildly curious. "What did they look like?" I asked, fully expecting to hear about halos and wings. " They really didn't look like anything. They were just very bright and they rushed from the back of the chapel out across the front. They seemed like they were in a hurry."

"How do you know they were angels?"

She looked at me blankly. "I just know they were."

"Why were they in a hurry?"

Now she was irritated with my probing. "I don't know. They just were."

By the way, the chapel is set in the woods, and I've never seen any daylight creep into it. I'm not repeating this story as proof of a supernatural sighting. I'm as cynical, and curious, as the next man. But like the mother who's daughter had bright people who visited her, I don't want to close the door on a subject I know nothing about. Not for me, and not for my child.

I don't know if exposure to our very concrete, real world is what saps the spiritual awareness out of us. We are too often grounded to what's real and perhaps not open enough to what's unreal—or not understood. So much of what is superior in life is untouchable and undefinable—love and art, for example. I believe man's need for art stems from the spiritual side of his nature. Art is a very spiritual expression. It is not science or physics; it has no laws or rules, and it is completely defined by the observer. Art is a need of the soul, not the body, and it is art that generates and exalts beauty. The older I get the more I appreciate a beautiful painting or a powerful symphony. Things that left me cold in youth suddenly have meaning for me.

When I began asking mothers if they felt any spiritual connection with their child, all but one woman gave me a very powerful yes. Many said they had trouble giving me an example, but that it was an overriding sense they had with their children. Here's what some of the mothers told me:

> With each of my children they seem to see to the center, the core of what is going on. They seem to have an old wisdom.

> I think you can only have a sense of spirituality with your child if you have it with yourself. I know with my family, we are on a path individually and as a group. We are pledged together.

> We are very spiritually connected. we read each other. Our connection is a bonding, and I think that unfortunately some parents use that for controlling instead of nurturing a child.

> This child is my late, very very loved late Nana. I have no doubt about that. This is so hard to explain. I look into her eyes and not only do I know her, she also knows me very, very well. We are not only two flesh-and-blood human beings playing together and holding hands, but we are also two little fairies floating above us who are very happy

to be together again.

Our daughter was conceived on our anniversary, and that has always felt very spiritual and blessed to me.

To look into my child's eyes, to feel the sense of continuum, that you do go on in their little souls somehow. It makes you feel a little bit immortal.

Our son was conceived on our wedding night, We'd been living together for years, and since it wasn't a planned pregnancy it was kind of like this little being had been hovering somewhere in space waiting for us to finally get married so he could be born.

What we learn from the birth of a child will vary for each of us depending on who we are, where we are in life, and the child that comes to you. If you believe, as I do, that we are all here to learn, then everything and everyone is a lesson. For me it has been exciting at my advanced age to become an eager student of life. How lovely that I was sent such a fascinating teacher—my child.

Chapter 24

In the End

In the middle of one recent night, when sleep was eluding me, I began replaying in my mind all the questions I'd been asking the mothers I was interviewing. Operating, I guess, out of a false assumption that I secretly knew my own answers, I had never bothered to question myself. But what I asked myself that night was the big question I hadn't even dared contemplate before. And that was, "Would I do this again, knowing all that I know now?" The immediate answer is yes. But with a big "however." The big "however" is that parenting is a much more enormous and life-changing experience than I think anyone is prepared for. Especially an older woman.

The receptionist at my dentist's office is back after her

three-month maternity leave and she couldn't wait to talk when I got there. "I can't believe how difficult this is. My husband and I are constantly fighting. I'm always in tears. I can't go anywhere without it being a major hassle, and if I *do* go anywhere I spend half the time worrying about the baby," and on and on. I assured her it would get better with time. What I didn't say was, "About three years, to be exact." When she told me of some of her upsets I recognized the pain and confusion of that time all over again and I knew what she was going through.

On the other hand, my daughter has brought me down to earth in a way I'd never before experienced. She provided me with the opportunity to be selfless in a selfish world. And the experiences that were so taxing for me during those first few years were the groundwork for what we now enjoy. Much the same as the effort expended by a farmer, I am now reaping what was sown. But like that farmer, I continue to rotate the crops for future harvests. There are more seasons ahead for both my child and me. I must constantly prepare for the future.

We all live in a world where we have grown to expect instant results, and I think I was unprepared for something that needed time to flourish. We have unfortunately been indoctrinated lately into thinking that everything is disposable. The only person we can't divorce is our child (or children). Many of us are not prepared as a society to put in the hard work it takes to create a family. We have been falsely lead to believe that good things come easily—that if something is meant to be, it just happens. Some have lost their ability to choose a higher good over immediate gratification. And the uncertainty with which we first begin to parent is uncomfortable for us to endure.

I didn't know that parenting would demand that I grow way up. Having kids makes you grow up. Much as a parent's death forces you to realize that you're the older generation now, so also does parenting raise your notch on the ladder of life. I'm not the baby anymore.

But all good things in life, all truly good things, take time and effort and love. I didn't truly know that before I had my baby. I needed the experience to teach me.

There were many unforgettable moments in the beginning. I can still remember how the baby smell was positively intoxicating. And I can remember the day I realized I could easily kill to protect her. Still now, I can recall what it felt like to have her moving around inside me. Now when I see her asleep, her long legs almost reaching the end of the bed, I marvel that she was ever inside me. What a gift life gave me.

So would I do it again? Yes, and yes again. I now really know how *precious* life is. During an interview with one late mother she said, almost in a whisper, "You know I really do believe in a woman's right to choose, but now that I have my baby, I can't *imagine* ever having an abortion." I understand her dual thinking.

Are older mothers better mothers? I think we are. I think our desire to parent, and parent well, is so strong that we do a better job of it than someone much younger. How could we not? We've had the added years to help us mature and grow and fulfill ourselves so that we recognize that giving to a child is a privilege. There is tremendous sweetness in tasting a pleasure so long denied. As older parents we are anxious to meet our obligations to the very best of our abilities. Our age makes us deeply cognizant of the gift that life truly is.

I look forward to the future (yes, even the teen years) to see who my daughter will become. My daughter has given me a future to look forward to—proms, graduations, a wedding perhaps, and, if God is willing, a grandchild someday to hold. Because just like my mother, I want my child to know the joy of holding, and loving, a child. It is the best thing in the world.

Resources

Adoptive Families of America
612-535-4829

FEMALE
(Formerly Employed Mothers at the Leading Edge)
P.O. Box 31
Elmhurst, IL 60126
708-941-3553

Mothers at Home
8310A Old Courthouse Rd.
Vienna, VA 22182
703-827-5903

National Adoptive Hotline
202-328-8072

Parentage (for the new parent over thirty-five)
19 West 21st St.
New York, NY 10010
212-924-9400
800-299-4818

Perinatal Health, Inc.
7777 Greenback Lane, Suite 205
Citrus Heights, CA 95610
800-562-4456

RESOLVE (Infertility and Adoption Information)
1310 Broadway
Sommerville, MA 02144-1731
617-623-0744

Single Mothers by Choice
P.O. Box 1642
Gracie Square Station
New York, NY 10028
212-988-0993

U.S. Department of Health and Human Services
National Adoptive Clearinghouse
202-842-1919